I change

A New Look at the *I Ching*

A guide to changing lives in changing times

Joanna Infeld

ISBN: 978-0-9979047-7-2

Printed in the United States of America

KO
RA

K O R A
P R E S S

"I must be willing to give up what I am
in order to become what I will be."

Albert Einstein (1879-1955)

Also by the author:

The 7 Ages of Woman
Dear Gabriel; Letters From a Trainee Angel
In-Formation; Moments of Realization
In-Tuition; Moments of Awakening
In-Sight; Moments of Being
A Garden of Qualities
God's Spies, Gratefully Aging
Behave Yourself; How to BE yourself and HAVE the life you want
The Tale of the Tailess Sperm
Unmasked; Spirit Flares

All available from www.Amazon.com and www.Korapress.com

Acknowledgements

Thank you to everyone who has been supportive when writing this book, especially my husband David Price Francis and Stephanie Morita who helped design some of the vignettes.

CONTENTS

CHANGE

Life is about change. Whatever age you are now, next year at this time you will be one year older. By the same token, last year at this time you were one year younger.

In ten years' time you will be a whole decade older. How do you feel about that? Are you prepared for the process of aging? This book can help you come to terms with constant change because it is all about change—that's what the *I* in Chinese means—change. *Ching* means book; therefore the *I Ching* is the *Book of Changes*.

There are internal changes and external changes; internal are more of a yin (feminine) nature, whereas external ones are more yang (masculine). Either can be dramatic or subtle, sudden or slow.

Change means transition—from one state to another. We are always in transition, never static or fixed, even if we might think we are settled and "home." Therefore, one hexagram can never define one's complete predicament; we must always look at the transition from where we are to where we are going. So we always work with two hexagrams—the first one defines our position at this time while the second one is where we are heading, what beckons, what is possible. It is an opportunity to be fulfilled, an opening that awaits, a position to move into. This book gives a basic understanding of each hexagram but does not interpret its placing next to each of the other hexagrams because there is a total of 4,032 possible readings when combining any two of the eight hexagrams (not to mention the fact that even two readings with the exact same two hexagrams will be interpreted differently for each person). Thus the possible number of *I Ching* readings is infinite. When placed next to each other, within the two hexagrams there are three possibilities for each of the six lines: each line either stays constant (this is a young line), or changes from yin to yang, or from yang to yin (a changing line is considered old). So change can be small (only one or two lines change from the first hexagram to the second), or even non-existent if none of the lines change and the first hexagram is the same as the second. If all lines change, it will mean that the person for whom the reading is performed is in a time of total transition and change.

The *I Ching* is a guidance during times of change. Since we are always transitioning from one state to another, the *I Ching* is always relevant. It points to a direction; it is then up to the person to decide what to do. The *I Ching* does not give advice; it is more like shining a light into a dark room, because we are always facing the unknown.In this analogy the future is the dark room.

When reading the *I Ching*, we throw three coins or anything that has two different sides to it. One side represents an unbroken line (usually heads, but if it is, say, a penny with the queen's head on it, heads will represent a broken line) and the tails will usually represent an unbroken line. The straight line is masculine in its nature (yang); the broken line is feminine (yin). To create a hexagram, each throw of the coins represents one line (broken or unbroken). Hexagrams are drawn from the bottom up, starting with the first line and then building the next five lines on top of the first. So each line will be represented by two heads and one tail (usually an unbroken line) or two tails and one head (usually a broken line).

When we draw each hexagram side-by-side, the first one represents where we are coming from, while the second is where we are heading toward. Our present moment is being in the middle, between the two. When we compare the two hexagrams, we will usually see that some lines remain the same and some lines will have changed, unless both hexagrams remain exactly the same, which is a very unusual occurrence, since each hexagram has only one in 64 chances to materialize. If it does happen, it will mean that the person is in a time of little change or stagnation.

HOW TO READ THE HEXAGRAMS

O nce the two hexagrams have been drawn, read descriptions for each and contemplate the movement from one state into the next. Additional insight can be gained by looking at the descriptions of all four trigrams that make up the two hexagrams.

YIN AND YANG

Yin (a broken line) and yang (an unbroken line) symbolize feminine and masculine energies. Everything in creation can be defined in terms of these two energies; everything possesses and radiates male and female energy—equal but different. In numerological terms, these two frequencies can be represented by the numbers one and two—one for the male energy and two for the female.

The unbroken yang line (masculine) is more fixed and stable; the female double line is more flexible, pliable and adaptable. However, both are subject to change and in a traditional reading of the *I Ching* either can be a stable (young) line or a changing (old) one.

YIN

The broken line represents the female energy or the number two. The female energy has two components within it, just as the female of the human species can house within it new life—it is the female who becomes pregnant and gives birth, thus causing the species to grow and multiply.

The number two surrounds and expounds the one, giving it definition and providing the ecology, the maintenance and the necessary continuance. The female energy is in its nature comforting, nurturing, surrounding, enveloping, providing and caring. These are words that belong with the female way, whether expressed by a man or a woman, for both take in and give out both forms of energy—masculine and feminine—though in different configurations.

Like the Earth, the woman is subject to cycles—the cycle of the moon defines her monthly ovulation cycle and the times of fertility. The cycle of years marks her age and defines the transition from the times of growing up, taking on responsibility, facing a renewed mid-life opportunity, to the ending of fertility—menopause—and the acquiring of wisdom in one's old age.

Like the Earth, the woman gives birth physically, mentally and spiritually, and her natural way is to give, nurture and to take care of others. The female archetype gives in abundance, always more than she receives. She is a planter of seeds. From small acorns mighty oak trees grow and a small seed can develop into plants, herbs, flowers, fruit or vegetables. She is also a provider, giving more than is needed, never counting the cost, always striving with each passing day for something better. Thus the female energy of the human species is more inclined toward stability, planning, security and foundation building.

YANG

The unbroken line represents the male energy, or the number one. The straight line is masculine in nature, transmissive and singular. Like the number one, the letter I, an arrow, the lingam and an obelisk point toward their destination, so the masculine energy aims at a tasking and strives toward perfection, with an urge and a calling never to stop. The man is the initiator and the male energy causes the beginning of all things. Thus the masculine energy (whether processed by a man or a woman) is the doer, the risk taker, the bringer of ideas and initiative.

It has been scientifically proven that men have greater tunnel vision than women, whereas women's peripheral vision is better developed than men's. Thus the male energy is better at becoming focused and single-minded, whereas women are good at picking up the stragglers and doing background checks to make sure everything is running smoothly.

WHAT IS A DIGRAM?

A hexagram consists of three digrams, which is yet another way of looking at the oracle. Each of the three sets of two lines represents one of the four possible combinations.

THE YIN AND YANG LINES TOGETHER
The four possible relationships between a single broken line (yin) and a single unbroken line (yang) are as follows: two unbroken lines, two broken lines, one unbroken line above a broken one, and one broken line above an unbroken one.

1. Both lines are unbroken (yang)
This is a masculine digram suggesting a double call to action. This digram represents a road or a river and defines a tasking, a project or a way in which a person does something. It is directed toward a result but it could also represent short-sightedness or a singular view.

2. Both lines are broken (yin)
This is a feminine digram that represents versatility, multiplicity and the ability to look at a situation or person in many different ways. A person who has this digram in their reading might be dispersed or unable to make a decision on the one hand, but capable of fairness and forgiveness on the other.

3. A broken line (yin) above an unbroken line (yang)
With firm foundations, this digram indicates that it is time to make a decision—faced with a choice the person is in a time of transition.
      Every day we face choices; every moment we choose what to think, how to be or what to do, and every moment these choices carry a consequence that in its turn leads to further choices. Everything a person wears, for example, is a choice. First it was a choice to buy it in amongst many other options at the store; then it was a choice to wear it on any particular day.
      This digram reminds a person to beware of their choices and not to make decisions lightly. It is important to remember that choices have consequences.

4. An unbroken line (yang) above a broken line (yin)
Here the foundations are twofold. They are not necessarily falling apart, because it could simply mean that there is a split loyalty, like, for example, looking after one's own family and one's aging parents, or being torn between the desire to do something that might take a person away from responsibility or duty, like wanting a new career but feeling the necessity to continue with one's current commitments. It might be that the person has a job that offers regular security and helps pay the bills, but offers little inspiration or satisfaction.

This digram could also represent the limitation of one's actions or points of view. It could mean that a person is being (temporarily) challenged in their pursuit of their goals.

WHAT IS A TRIGRAM?

A trigram is a figure consisting of three lines, each one of which is either unbroken (yang) or broken (yin). Each hexagram consists of two trigrams, or two figures of three lines, one placed on top of the other.

There are eight possible trigrams in the *I Ching*: heaven, earth, water, fire, thunder, wind, mountain and lake.

1. HEAVEN

Three unbroken lines
Heaven is a trigram representing strength, inspiration and creativity. It also relates to a person's faith and spiritual endeavor. It can also indicate ambition, high ideals and lofty goals.

2. EARTH

Three broken lines

Earth is a trigram representing change, cycles and firm foundations. It also represents variety and multiple choices, as well as hesitation and uncertainty.

3. WATER

An unbroken line between two broken lines
Water is a life giving force. It washes away the
past and brings nourishment and sustenance
in preparation for the future. Water also
represents one's emotions and is a harbinger
of change.

4. FIRE

A broken line between two unbroken lines

Fire can be destructive but with control it can
be warming and cleansing. It brings inspiration
and connects a person to the creative muses. In a
reading it signals the need for containment and
points to a powerful creative energy, waiting to find
its expression and release.

5. THUNDER

Two broken lines above an unbroken line
Thunder is a prelude to a storm; it announces
sweeping changes. With firm foundations, one
can easily weather the coming changes. In a
reading it suggests the need to relook at one's
commitments, goals and priorities.

6. WIND

Two unbroken lines above a broken line
Wind causes changes—it blows in new
frequencies and new possibilities. It
suggests that there is a need to look to
one's foundations and "batten down
the hatches." It also suggests that although a person might be very
confident in their actions, their motives need reinforcement. It
reminds the reader that nothing in their environment is permanent
and everything is subject to change—possessions, relationships,
careers and the feeling of wellbeing.

7. MOUNTAIN
One unbroken line above two broken lines

The mountain represents aspirations and inspirations. It is also an obstacle on the way that needs to be climbed in order to view and get to your next destination. It can be seen as a test or an invitation. When approaching a mountain, you can only see one side of it, but when you have reached the peak, a whole new vista opens up before you. So the future might seem uncertain, but it will reveal itself in time. Therefore one needs to look to one's staminas and wellbeing to be able to successfully take on the obstacles that lie ahead.

8. LAKE
One broken line above two unbroken lines

A lake is a depository of power; it symbolizes a person's deeper feelings and desires. Its power can remain hidden, but when unleashed it is a force to be reckoned with. In a reading it suggests the need for a time of meditation, intraspection and deeper self knowledge. It could mean there are issues in one's psyche that are being avoided or "swept under the carpet."

WHAT IS A HEXAGRAM?
A hexagram is a figure consisting of three digrams, two trigrams, or six lines. There are 64 possible combinations of two trigrams where each line is either broken or unbroken.

As with any personal reading, there are many possible interpretations of each hexagram. Each reading involves an understanding of two hexagrams and the possible interpretations are endless. When reading the *I Ching* it is important to take into account the situation of the person whose reading is being attempted—everyone is unique and no two readings will ever be the same, even if two people have exactly the same two hexagrams in their readings. The *I Ching* is a tool with which one can help another (or oneself) come to a deeper understanding of one's situation at any given time.

The *I Ching* is a key to a person's soul. It is important to treat it with respect because it can cause a person to feel naked, exposed, and vulnerable. It is also a great help in clarifying one's situation and reaching difficult, as well as not-so-difficult, decisions.

The Hexagrams

The Hexagrams

Upper → / Lower ↓	Heaven	Thunder	Water	Mountain	Earth	Wind	Fire	Lake
Heaven	1	34	5	26	11	9	14	41
Thunder	25	51	3	27	24	42	21	17
Water	6	40	29	4	7	59	64	47
Mountain	33	62	39	52	15	53	56	31
Earth	12	16	8	23	2	20	35	45
Wind	44	32	48	18	46	57	50	28
Fire	13	55	63	22	36	37	30	49
Lake	10	54	60	41	19	61	38	58

1. CREATIVITY
Heaven below, Heaven above

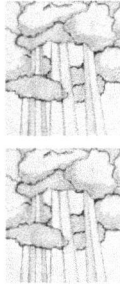

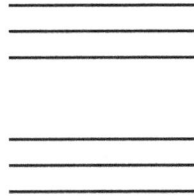

The first symbol of the *I Ching* represents initiation, initiative and inspiration. It is the universal beginning where all great works and inventions start—in the energy worlds, with a single thought and a powerful inspiration. All great discoveries and creative processes can be traced back to a single moment, to a thought that dawns like a bolt of lightning. Such a moment changes everything that comes afterward.

This inspiration can give rise to a new project, an enterprise, or a new relationship. Everything in a person's history builds up to that moment. Then it is as if a new threshold is crossed and new vistas open up. The build up is slow and hard to see, but the change brought about by these beginnings can be dramatic, like an overnight success or a love affair that begins with a first sighting of one's loved one.

Inspiration brings joy and purpose and is as close as a person can get to experiencing heaven while living on Earth. The feeling of being moved to action is pure and powerful, and its consequent unfolding can last a lifetime.

It is the way the divine speaks to us—giving us a glimpse of what is possible and then allowing us to implement our right to choose the ways and means in which we prefer to act, or not, as the case might be.

Inspiration is a gift from the gods, not to be squandered. It is like a package of energy supplied when we least expect it. It is then our privilege and prerogative to unpack this potent package and use the energy delivered to create something new that can inspire others.

The unfolding of our gift can happen fast or slow, or we can even choose to ignore it. But if we do, this might be a signal sent to the universal powers that delivered it in the first place that we are not interested in further inspiration, and it therefore might be a while before we receive another such gift (if at all).

It is always best to acknowledge a gift and plan how you intend to use it. Gifts from heaven are very deliberately targeted and inspiration usually comes moulded to fit the receiver's skills and abilities. Thus a painter will receive a visual inspiration, while a writer will be moved by a subject to write about, and a musician will hear a sequence of notes in his or her head.

To prepare for this great gift—inspiration—it is important to know what inspires and moves you so the sender can recognize your desires and deliver an appropriate response. If a writer spends his or her time writing, and a painter paints with dedication and commitment, even before they are inspired, then they are preparing to receive the greatest gift of all.

Waiting for inspiration is not enough. It is important to hone one's skills and be found pottering about in the territory within which one wishes to find inspiration. Inspiration is there, waiting for the right person to ring the right tuning fork tuned to the right frequency for inspiration to drop in and move its new host to action.

Great musicians who wrote divinely inspired work—Beethoven, Bach, Mozart—loved their music and kept exercising their craft until they were inspired to write such elevated works as *The Ninth Symphony*, the *Brandenburg Concerto* and *The Magic Flute* respectively. Many classical writers invoked their muse before beginning to write. They believed that their inspiration came from a higher energetic source.

Not everyone is as talented as the great composers, writers or painters, but we all have at least one talent which can help us lead an inspired life. It might be helping others, designing websites or cooking a meal. Within all specializations there is room for creativity which brings joy and a sense of fulfillment. This is how life progresses and evolution happens.

Inspiration is the bringer of true originality—a new frequency and energy that is seeking entry into planet Earth. Somewhere somebody is on the frequency of this new energy to become midwife to its arrival. It might just be you. To be creative is the closest a human can get to the idea of being a creator or a co-creator. We humans are potentially producers of originality if we are able to respond to the original signals arriving here from the universe.

Creativity brings joy, satisfaction and happiness. It opens new channels for energy to flow through; it inspires and causes further produce. Each life is entitled to be creative. Each life has the possibility to express itself in its own unique way. Once a person discovers what that way is, they can find fulfillment and happiness in what they do.

The easiest way to connect to higher energy is to become creative, in whatever capacity is appropriate for each person. We are born to be creative and everyone has the ability to find that creative vein that will allow him or her to become inspired by what they do.

Our understanding of God, or a higher being, is of someone or some power that is creative. He, she, it has created the human being and all the animals of the field, fish of the sea and birds of the air. How creative this force must be to create such successful life forms that have managed to survive throughout centuries, despite wars, famine and natural disasters!

Being creative elevates us to a higher vibration. Inspired by our works we have no time or energy to waste on depression or worry. A creative person will be drawn to their creativity because it will be a source of joy, inspiration and spiritual happiness.

Thus, to be spiritually happy a person needs to find that special activity or thought process that is creative. It will energize them and help keep them healthy. It will bring them closer to those energy realms where muses, divas, angelic formations and fairies reside. This might sound like fantasy, but if you try it, you will surely see some amazing results.

When this hexagram appears in a reading, it signals a new beginning and a new initiative, and it instructs a person to follow their dreams. It ttells us that we should look for our inspiration by developing our unique skills, and by loving what we do.

The Oracle says:
A wise person is always grateful to the Creator and makes a consistent effort to become creative himself or herself.

Exercise
Write down three activities or processes that inspire you. Make sure that each week for four weeks you dedicate some time (say, at least one hour) to each of these activities. Note how you feel after each one and decide which one makes you happiest. Then spend the next 52 weeks dedicating much of your spare time to that activity or process. See if after one year has gone by you are not more inspired, happier and satisfied with your life.

2. RECEPTION
Earth below, Earth above

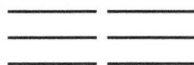

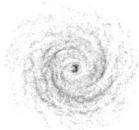

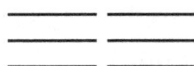

nitial inspiration becomes void if it is not received and followed up with action. Once a book is written or a symphony is composed, it needs to find its reader and its listener. What use is the best story if no one hears it and it is never told?

Earth receives the life-giving rays of the sun. The rays of the sun are only life-giving because they are received. Otherwise they would disperse into space and there would be nobody or nothing to utilize the solar energy and to bring into the light the results of photo-synthesis and the transmutation of solar power into material, energetic and spiritual produce.

A sun salutation is a response to the benefaction of the solar disc here on Earth. Without the planets in our solar system, the sun would have nowhere to lodge its produce—the heat and light—dispersed by its messenger rays.

Planet Earth receives energies from the universe and from the solar system; it is therefore influenced by all the planets that revolve around the sun. These energies were recognized in Egypt and in Babylon where each day was said to be influenced by a different planet. That is why in English, Spanish and in French we have names of the days of the week derived from the names of the planets of the ancients:

Monday (Lundi, lunes) for the moon
Tuesday (Mardi, martes) for Mars
Wednesday (Mercredi, miercoles) for Mercury
Thursday (Jeudi or Thor's day, jueves) for Jupiter

Friday (Vendri, viernes) for Venus
Saturday for Saturn
Sunday for the sun.

Each day, according to the Babylonians, there a primary, secondary and tertiary planetary influence, each in turn arriving at 12 midnight, 8a.m. and 4p.m. respectively, weakening as the day wears on. The prime influence which arrives at midnight comes in at full strength, at 100%. As this first influence weakens, the secondary influence arrives at 8a.m. with 50% of strength, and the third at 4p.m. introduces only a 25% additional power, the other two influences remaining effective as well as the day wears on.

	Mon	Tue	Wed	Thu	Fri	Sat	Sun
100%	Moon	Mars	Mercury	Jupiter	Venus	Saturn	Sun
50%	Saturn	Sun	Moon	Mars	Mercury	Jupiter	Venus
25%	Jupiter	Venus	Saturn	Sun	Moon	Mars	Mercury

The planet receives energy from all organic life, including the human. She needs higher energies for her maintenance and growth. It is a reciprocal maintenance, as she supports all the living beings who live upon her, feed from her and collect her planetary energies on her behalf.

Each person is a receiving station. Apart from receiving food, water, air and energy from the planet on which we live, we also receive the words spoken to us by others; we receive the feelings of those who are close to us, and we receive energy from the universe. Are we always conscious of these many gifts? Perhaps not, but we can take a moment in our busy day and think of ourselves as the receptors of food, energy, creative thoughts and inspiring ideas.

Inspiration is all around us. But when we are preoccupied with other things, like memories of the past, or worries about the future, we can miss the gifts that are being bestowed upon us every minute of every day.

Humans have the special ability to connect to higher energies, which neither flora nor fauna life can do. Animals and plants are planetary responders, but the human can connect to the energies of the sun, the stars, the galaxies, all the way through the Milky Way to the star belts and even higher up the ray of creation to what the Egyptians called the fields of peace.

When this hexagram appears in a reading, it is a reminder of our human station, as defined by our potential and possibility. It is a reminder that we are the receptors of high energies, but to become conscious of these transmissions, we need to sometimes become quiet inside and learn to attune our faculties to universal frequencies and change.

The Oracle says:
Remember that as a human you are naturally connected to many sources of food, including fine energies that originate from the universe.

Exercise:
Take a week to observe the changes in the energies of the day, as the frequency of a new day arrives at midnight or as the morning swings into full acton around 8a.m. Try to identify the different energetic hallmarks of each day of the week. How does Monday energy feel, as opposed to Sunday? What does the middle of the week feel like when Wednesday arrives? Which day brings the most energy and which is the quietest, inspiring more inward contemplations and reflections?

3. THE BEGINNING
Thunder below, Water above

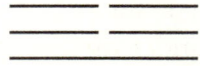

Once the heaven and the Earth are in place, and once the male and female principles are brought into being and established—something can begin. Whether it is a love affair, the birth of a child, or even just a simple conversation or the sharing of ideas—the foundations have been built and the two ingredients already established are begging for continuance and for usage. As in the yin/yang symbol—a little bit of heaven can be found on Earth, just as a little bit of Earth is reflected in the heavens. This ensures that each will be forever searching for its completion by looking for it in the other. The higher part of woman has been lodged in the man, just as the higher part of man has been lodged in the woman. Both a woman and a man are forever searching for their higher part. Even if a woman is single, lonely or celibate, she will still be searching for her higher part which is contained within the masculine energetic matrix. Likewise, the man is also always searching for his higher part. No matter where he is or what he is doing, the search continues unabated.

The great secret of the universe is that neither man nor woman, male nor female can ever be complete and fulfilled. The system has been rigged so there is perpetual motion between the two different types of energy expressed by men and women, though both genders can be in receipt of, process, and express both kinds of energy. Humans are forever searching for completion but as long as they are alive on planet Earth, they will never find it, except in brief moments. Once the moment is gone, a person will realize how elusive it had been and will be forever seeking another energetic fulfillment. So, there are moments when it feels like maybe this is it, but then the next moment arrives and the search continues for something still better and even more fulfilling.

This third symbol of the *I Ching* is the perfect storm—thunder and rain—that makes the yin/yang symbol come to life and spin. All over the world teenagers awaken to the existence of the other gender and their complementary energy, and begin pining for their missing part. This interaction between heaven and Earth, between the masculine and the feminine, between the yin and the yang, makes the world go round. It is responsible for romance, great literature and poetry, love songs and the deepest feelings of longing.

There is always something unfulfilled as we try to grab hold of our higher part lodged in another. Although we can experience it briefly during our love making or with our heartfelt exchanges, we can never really possess it or keep it. We remain hungry and incomplete—always seeking the next encounter or the next adventure.

A man or a woman's search for their higher part can take all kinds of forms. It does not need to be the quest for a lover or a life partner. It can turn up as a religious pursuit, a need for spirituality, or a hunger for adventure and new thrills. The conviction that our higher part lies waiting at the top of a mountain after an arduous hike, or within the covers of a published book we have written, or between the sheets with a loved one are all manifestations of the same desire for fulfillment that will never be completely satisfied. If it is, it will only appear for brief moments to then taunt us with its memory and with the permanent accompaniment of a desire for it to happen again.

When heaven comes to Earth, the rains fall and the water fertilizes the ground. As new life springs forth, symbolized by a blade of grass pushing through the surface of the ground in springtime, there is accompanying thunder and drama.

The beginnings of things are always difficult, whether starting a business enterprise or a love affair. Introducing a new energy into one's life always requires sacrifice—something has to give, to be able to receive the new. By the same token, in order to get rid of something old, like a bad habit or an addiction, it is best to replace the unwanted energy with something new—a new energy and a new initiative.

New energy entering our life requires new behaviors and new responses. Initiatives require the investment of a new effort and a new energy. Like learning a new language or how to drive a car, when we start something new, we feel awkward and uncertain at first. It is to be expected. We cannot start a new relationship and expect it to be brilliant from the beginning. In a new relationship it will take time to learn about the other person, their habits, ways, likes, dislikes. It is a wise person who is careful at the beginning of a new affair, as they learn to share their hopes, fears and experiences.

When starting a new job it takes time to remember everyone's name, to learn where everything is filed and to master the electronic devices, like the computer software, the copier and the fax machine. Then slowly, as time passes, one becomes more familiar with the environment and one soon learns who one can ask for help or advice and who tends to be unwilling to spare the time or energy to help one on one's journey of discovery.

A seed needs to be watered and fed to grow into a full-grown plant or tree; likewise, the beginning of a new project or implementing a life change can be arduous. It brings a person out of their comfort zone into new territory. This initiative is a great opportunity to learn about oneself and to challenge oneself. The key is to not mind the difficulties at the beginning but to keep going, to soldier on until the new situation becomes better established. However, when this happens (the settling down into a new situation), it might turn out to be time to move on and to find a new challenge, so that one is never too familiar with one's life and its evolving circumstances.

In a reading this hexagram signifies a new situation, whether it is a relationship, a job, a career or a new project. It encourages the person to not give up (at least not yet), and to weather the storm, as it will lead to new opportunities and new challenges later.

The Oracle says:
A new storm brings change and fresh energy into any situation. There is new opportunity on the horizon. You are entering into new territory and need to be vigilant about its requirements upon you. Whatever your new initiative, make sure you give it its due time and energy if you hope for it to bear fruit.

Exercise
Try something you have never tried before, like a new sport or a new skill. It can be walking down the street in slow motion or simply changing your stride. Observe yourself as you do so—how do you feel? Do you feel awkward or silly? Can you find ways to enjoy the new experience and overcome the feeling of being self-conscious? This exercise will help prepare you for what lies ahead and the many new situations and demands you will encounter in your future life.

4. YOUTHFUL FOLLY
Water below, Mountain above

Once the beginning is established—learning and growth follow. In a person's life this is the time of youth when they are daily experiencing something new and coming to understand the way of the world. A stream emerges as a spring from the depth of the mountain and flows downward, toward the valley below, gathering soil and water until it swells into a river by the time it reaches sea level.

This hexagram speaks of learning and the gathering of life experience. Where there is youth, there is also a teacher or mentor willing to impart his or her knowledge. Both student and teacher learn from the experience of sharing; both are enriched by the education that passes between them.

Just as the young man is foolish, so is the young woman foolish. A young person may look grown up and behave with refinement and sophistication, but there is no substitute for life experience and the wisdom of maturity. In our youth we are still learning the art of life, the ability to be a good mother or father, a loyal friend, a devoted husband or wife. All these roles are new, and as long as the young person knows that there is still a lot to learn, they can be successful in all their tasks.

Every parent learns to be a parent by experimenting with their children—there is no shortcut to wisdom, and experience is the best teacher. The qualities that can help a person gain confidence and efficiency in a new situation are humility, awareness, and the desire to learn. The image of a mountain stream represents the flow of life—gathering speed and volume as it descends from its source near the mountain top, gaining experience, fast or slow, depending on the incline of the mountain face and the volume of water.

"Don't try to run before you can walk" would be an appropriate saying here and another one would be, "to go with the flow." This does not mean giving up or handing over one's decision making capability to others. However, it does indicate that everything has its natural timing and to go against it could spell the difference between success and failure.

It takes nine months for a baby to be born and a young mother-to-be, waiting to give birth, should not become impatient. The experience of pregnancy is a unique opportunity to really connect with the growing life inside her, to feel its pulse, its character and needs. Once born, a child will demand her attention and her time to the exclusion of almost everything else, so pregnancy is a time to appreciate the nature of confinement—her last chance (at least for a while) to have time for herself, to contemplate the future and prepare for birth.

A young man or woman stepping into the world of responsibility needs to realize that he or she has to work for what he or she receives. It takes time to build a career, to develop life skills and to be good at what one does. For both a man and a woman each stage of life offers new opportunities and new experiences. As we move through time, time influences us, challenges us and molds us into the character we become as a result of our unique life journey.

A young person, whether male or female, venturing into the world also needs to learn to be patient. It takes time to learn a skill, to establish a successful career and to develop lasting relationships. Often a young person wants to see immediate results, as they set their feet upon the path of a new project or become involved in a new love affair. The antidote to the folly of youth is to build patience as part of one's character formation and to learn to develop a long view regarding one's desires and aims.

This hexagram warns about the need for an in-breath and a re-evaluation of one's position regarding a new opportunity or a new relationship. In a reading, this hexagram suggests we should value the age we are currently experiencing and the time we have to become who and what we want to be. This hexagram indicates the need for patience, both with oneself and with other people who influence one's life.

The Oracle says:
Your time is now. Use it wisely—it is a most precious gift. Look again at your intentions. Do not intend too much at any one time. Give yourself time to finish one project before you take on too many commitments at once.

Exercise

Picture a mountain and imagine that climbing it, and then descending, represents your life journey. Depending on your age, place yourself part way up the mountain, while ascending to the top represents mid-life, or the ages between 33 and 44. Imagine the view from wherever you happen to be and realize that you can only really see the descent after you reach your middle years. Realize that wherever you are on your life's journey, it is up to you to shape your future path to be anything you want it to be.

5. NEED
Heaven below, Water above

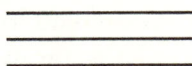

We are all needy. We are born needy. Everything that is new and fragile requires sustenance in order to grow. The child needs to be fed and kept warm, but above all it needs energy and its parents' love. We continue to be needy throughout our life as we require a continuous supply of energy and food.

Energy is the highest food of the five foods because we cannot live without it. We can live without physical food the longest—many days, depending on health and age. We can live for a few days without water, again depending on temperature, humidity and health. We can only survive for a few minutes without the third food—air. The fourth food is light and the fifth—the most important of all—is energy. We need all five foods to survive: solids, liquids, air, light and energy.

EARTH FOOD

There are many theories about the kind of food we should be eating—fashionable new diets come and go, new super foods are discovered on a regular basis and more and more people are becoming vegans, vegetarians or believers in a raw food diet.

LIQUID FOOD

We are made up mostly of water and cannot survive without the life-giving liquid for longer than a few days. As we have learned from *Messages From Water* by Dr. Masaru Emoto, the quality of our water can dramatically vary, depending on the source from which it comes, as well as the thoughts and emotions that go into the liquids we drink prior to ingesting them. (This goes for solids or earth food as well, which would explain why "Mom's cooking always tastes best," and why in many countries of the world the food is blessed before it is eaten.)

Water has become an important preoccupation in the last years as we tend to shun polluted tap water and drink either filtered or bottled water instead. Unfortunately, what this has precipitated is a huge surplus of plastic bottles on planet Earth, many of which are floating somewhere in the oceans as part of large masses of trash. We are just now beginning to be more aware of the damage being done to our environment and the planet by this huge collection of plastic, and we are finally finding ways to recycle and reuse, producing tiles, bags and even jewelry out of discarded plastic. The concern of the environmentalists is that all these efforts are too little too late.

AIR FOOD

Air is mostly not appreciated as much as water, yet in most parts of the world it is becoming a valued commodity which is becoming more and more polluted. Fresh air is beginning to be accessible only at a premium. In Tokyo, where pollution is extreme, there are machines where for a few yen a person can purchase a gulp of fresh air. It is quite likely that such machines will be coming to other cities in the world as well soon. Certainly Los Angeles, Beijing or Mexico City, where smog levels are high, could benefit from such an amenity.

LIGHT FOOD

Light comes to us from the sun. It is a known fact that in northern countries and states where sunlight considerably diminishes in the winter, like Sweden and Washington State, depression rates and the suicide statistics are higher (in Washington State the suicide rate was 14 per 100,000 in 2011—well over the national average of 10.1). Without sunlight no green plant or tree would grow. Sunlight is a life-giving force without which we would perish. It has been proven that to counteract the lack of sunlight, the use of full spectrum lighting provides the necessary frequencies to lift a person's mood.

(Interesting that a mood can be either dark or light.)

ENERGY FOOD

The most important food is energy and the human race is finally awakening to the fact that there are many levels and various qualities to this most precious food.

Everything is energy—our thoughts, our emotions, our conversations, our relationships, our wants and our desires. We humans tend to vacillate between higher and lower energies, depending on our experience, thought patterns and moods. There are seven levels of energy. Starting at the low end of level seven, this is where the energies of crime and perversion can be found. There are six other levels of energy a human can connect to. At level six are the energies of daily life that are responsible for our maintenance, grooming and habitual actions. At level five are energies associated with learning and self-improvement. At level four a person connects to healing energies and the energies associated with such qualities as generosity, care, patience and selflessness. At level three one becomes open to the energies of nature spirits, devi, elementals and angels. At the highest two levels a human can lift their thoughts to reach for the stars and connect to the energies of the universe. These two higher levels have given rise to all the major world religions.

We are surrounded by energy; everything emanates and processes energy. From birth to death we live, act and grow within a bubble of energy called the aura. Everything else that lives on planet Earth is surrounded by energy as well, but their energy takes the shape of the being or the object from which it emanates— whether animal, vegetable, mineral or man-made. For example, a tree emanates energy; this energy radiates away from the tree and blends into the Earth's atmosphere. It is not held within a bubble like the human aura, but dissipates to join the energy fields of the planet. Human energy stays contained within the egg-shaped aura and dissipates only very slowly, unless the aura is punctured either deliberately or through disease, negative thoughts or emotions, or general malaise.

When we think of a person who is at distance, we send a

thin wire of energy that travels to that person. If they are clairvoyant and sensitive enough, they might pick it up consciously and spare a moment or a fleeting thought about us in return. Sometimes we might find ourselves thinking of someone and then within minutes, or even seconds, they will phone us, or contact us by texting. When we speak with another person, shake hands with them or exchange eye contact, we are exchanging energy. Some exchanges are more powerful than others and sometimes we can feel the look of another person as a wave of force that can either enhance our state or cause the opposite—upset or irritation.

Everything is energy—words, conversations, looks, touch, sex. We need our daily supply of energy in order to survive. On the whole women are more susceptible to the more subtle shades of an energetic exchange. They can also be more vulnerable and more at a loss when they do not receive the energy they crave. Men, on the other hand, are better at preserving their energy because they are less prone to giving it away to any needy person they happen to encounter.

A baby thrives on its mother's touch as well as her milk. The mother receives from the child energetic confirmation of the baby's dependency, which reassures her about her own importance in the child's life. As the child grows into its teenage years and becomes more independent, so the reduction of energy flow from the child to the mother can cause a woman to question her self-worth. This is a time for a woman to begin to reconnect to her own fullness by rediscovering what it is that brings her inspiration and satisfaction. As teenagers turn to friends, boyfriends or girlfriends for their supply of energy, so a parent needs to find their energetic fulfillment elsewhere.

Energy needs continue throughout life, but in the natural course of aging a person becomes less dependent on outside stimuli and is more self-reliant as they can learn to connect to universal energies that are abundantly available on planet Earth. This is done by finding one's path and purpose and following its course. Easier said than done, and sometimes it takes a lifetime of search to find one's inspiration and calling.

This hexagram refers to our needs and to the fact that with every decision we make, we must make sure that we have access to the five foods to guarantee continuance. It also indicates that although our needs demand to be filled, it is our choice how we ensure the supply of the five foods and at what level we choose to connect to the energies that will bring satisfaction and fulfillment. This hexagram reminds us of our humanity and the need to aspire to higher energies that are readily available in our day-to-day life. What you take into yourself in the form of the five foods will determine what you are able to produce and create as you follow your chosen path.

The Oracle says:
Be careful what you eat and what level of energy you connect to as you go about your day. Every thought, emotion and action brings with it a new energy and a new opportunity to lift oneself up to higher energy realms.

Exercise:
Fast for a day (24 hours), drinking only water. Register your value for your first meal after the fast.

Hold your breath for as long as you can, then breathe in the air deeply. Call over your value for the air.

6. CONFLICT
Water below, Heaven above

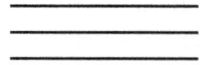

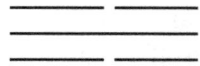

There is no human life without conflict. There is no great literature and no story to be told that does not incorporate the emergence and resolution of conflict.

Where there are two or more people gathered, inevitably a difference of opinion must arise. No two people think alike, have the same experiences, or favor the same actions.

The natural worlds of plants, trees and minerals are not in conflict with their environment. Animals might have territorial struggles or fight to win a mate, but they do not argue about who is right and who is wrong. They have no philosophical discussions or disagreements about art or science. They do not initiate religious wars or political persecution.

Children experience conflict in life early on. It might be a disagreement about a toy, or an upset because a parent wanted the child to do something the child did not feel like doing. Conflict can also be internal—the conflict between duty and pleasure, or between divided loyalties when, for example, we are torn between wanting to please two different people who have requested our support at the same time.

Where there is life, there is conflict. It cannot be prevented; it is the means of our growth and can become a learning and a development exercise. Conflict teaches us about ourselves and reflects back to us the qualities of our character, depending on how we handle it. Conflict is the very bloodline of progress—without doubt, and questioning, and conflict there is no striving for what is true and no possibility to find improvement in any situation. So welcome conflict as your teacher and your guide, but attempt to be neutral and impartial, so that anger and hurt do not impede your judgment. Would you not want to greet a teacher in an open and ready to proceed manner?

Conflict is part of life and there is no growth without it. It is within the battleground between two views, two modes of behavior, two loyalties or two opinions that we discover who we are and define our adherence to one side or the other. Being born into a particular family, race, nation and religion, as well as a system of beliefs about ourselves and the world, we are handed down and taught about our identity so we can embrace it and fill it out. We then have the choice to accept it or not, to take that identity and wear it like a badge, or to question it, redefine it, or decide to become someone quite different. Some aspects, like gender and race, are fixed at birth, but our beliefs about who we are and who we might become are flexible and open to change. This is one of the great challenges and privileges of being human—the ability and the requirement to change. We never stay the same from moment to moment and from one age to the other. We are always growing in experience and wisdom, and every day provides new opportunities for self discovery and for building character.

Conflict is part of this process. It is a double-sided mirror that reflects back to us our side of the story, while at the same introducing another view or another way of looking at situations and other people. It is an opportunity to extend one's views and consider an alternative, to be able to perhaps arrive at a third way that can become a solution and a resolution to the conflict.

Men think differently to women and their energy systems are wired differently. In any man/woman relationship, whether in marriage or at work, there are bound to be misunderstandings, differences of opinion and conflicting views. Each of these situations is an opportunity to grow and learn about each other.

It is important to approach conflict with respect for the other person and to embrace it, rather than resent it. Eventually every resolved conflict becomes water under the bridge and part of the history of joint experiences, which will feed into the wealth of shared references and joint folklore for years into the future.

Conflict is part of life and part of every relationship within which energies between people are exchanged; it proves we are alive. There will always be certain rubbings, misunderstandings, disagreements, hurts, differences of opinion, the clashings of different desires and goals—all of which can lead to a renewed commitment, a better understanding and tighter bonds between people.

Conflict does not need to be painful. Every altercation or disagreement is an opportunity to learn about oneself or another person. We should be grateful that other people think differently from us—that we can learn from them and expand our own world view. If everyone thought like we do, the world would be a boring place and we would have no one to talk to to share our views, opinions and ideas, because everyone would already know them and agree with them.

To embrace conflict is to become open to alternative views, which perhaps are better founded than our own. It allows us to grow as humans and learn about other people in the process. A conflict of interest can arise when two people want the same thing but there is only room for one to achieve it, like when two people compete for a job, or when two men are in love with the same woman. In the case of rivalry for a position or new job, the boss decides who is a better candidate for the position; in the case of the two men competing for the affection of one woman, she will ultimately be the deciding principle, when she lets it be known who is her favorite.

In a reading this hexagram points to the need to embrace conflict, rather than trying to avoid it. It suggests that conflict, once resolved, is not as daunting as at the time when it first arises. Usually this points to the need for communication. Conflict, once brought out into the open, loses its power; when both parties value each other and are willing to speak and negotiate, resolution cannot be far away. It suggests approaching the person with whom the conflict has arisen with respect and honesty, and to talk out your grievances until a resolution is found and implemented.

The Oracle says:

The conflict you are experiencing—whether internal or external—can lead to a resolution that is progressive and beneficial, if you let it play out and take its natural course. Do not force the result; you will know what to do when the time is right.

If you can, try to go to sleep at night clear and free of conflict, whether internal strife or external disagreement with another person.

Exercise:
Write down a list of people you do not feel clear with, for whatever reason. Call them or write to them and present to them your viewpoint, while asking them for theirs. Listen attentively and see if you can either agree with them or agree to disagree.

7. THE ARMY
Water below, Earth above

With eight billion people on the planet, we are almost always surrounded by people. Unless we go and live as a recluse, or find a cave on top of a mountain somewhere, we are likely to be influenced by the energy exchange with people, whether on Zoom, at work, at home, or on the street.

Groups of people can be a valuable support system for the individual, but they can also generate group conformity and deprive a person of their originality and creativity.

Teenage years are a time of learning to deal with others socially and in other group settings, but it is also a time of rebellion when a young person learns to think for himself or herself. It is a time to question authority and to realize that not everything we are taught in school or were told by our parents is in fact true.

Then in later years, during the time of establishing oneself independently away from the parental home, one becomes busy with a career, with further education, building relationships, managing finances, and perhaps setting up a home. A job, a relationship, becoming a parent—all these changes demand acquiescence to another's way and style, tolerance and becoming a team player. It would seem that the rebellious years are over, once one reaches the early twenties, or when these new relationships are formed and strengthened.

But then comes the mid-life crisis or, as perhaps it should be known, the mid-life opportunity. This is a new kind of rebellion—one in which a person questions their own choices so far. It is a time to look to the future and reshape one's ambitions, aims and plans.

This is a time of many changes, of learning from past experiences and of hopes for the future—deciding who one is and who one has the possibility of becoming. All these times of transition—the teenage years, becoming independent and the mid-life opportunity—are also times to re-examine one's character and to build one's energetic arsenal to be able to face any future situation life might present us with in the future.

To be prepared to fight a war and to win in any situation, a person needs two very important weapons in their arsenal: their skills and their qualities. We never have enough of either and will spend our lives accumulating both.

Skills are our various abilities—the things we can do. Everything we do on a regular basis adds to our skill level, because as we repeat an action, we become better at it. Nothing is ever perfect, so always improvements can be made. It is important to not become complacent and to always be in training. Even the things we do at a professional level—the actions and skills we are paid for—can always be improved, refined, developed and added to. A writer can become a better writer, a mother can improve her mothering abilities, and a teacher can learn from his or her students how to become a better teacher.

Our qualities are those attributes that we have managed to distill from our experience of living so that they become the very essence of our character formation. Thus, by exercising patience repeatedly and over time, we will eventually become a patient person, in whom the quality of patience resides and is available to spring into action at any time. A patient person cannot help but be patient and have patience at the ready, like a sword in its sheath. However, there can also be times when patience is not needed, but the situation requires for the person to exercise haste and quick decisions. The hallmark of a person who has a quality at their disposal, as part of their character formation, is the fact that they can choose to use it or not, because it is always there, forever ready and forever faithful.

In order to live a life of quality, one can deliberately decide to develop one's character and identity to include certain qualities, or virtues, as they used to be called. These can range from courage to generosity, to compassion, to serenity and a million of others. Some people grow up in a home where, for example, sharing is a way of life. It might be easy for such a person to become host to the quality of generosity in later years. However, anyone can activate any quality by deliberately researching and meditating upon its characteristics and energetic frequency. Like goes to like and you draw to yourself what you think about. The quickest and most effective way to connect to a quality is to act with it in mind, to deliberately put oneself on its frequency. Therefore a courageous act will make a person more courageous. To connect to patience, for example, one would need to act with patience; to become compassionate one would act and think with compassion. After a while, the energy of one's chosen quality or qualities will come to reside in one's energy field and become recognized by all whom one encounters.

This hexagram suggests that a person can deliberately and consciously set one's feet upon the path of becoming a person of quality. It also suggests that a person might want to define who they are and decide to empower their character by adding to their skill set and to their range of qualities.

The Oracle says:
Consider your army and your staff. What are your skills and what qualities define your character? Now is a good time to reconsider who and what you want to become and to set your feet upon the path of becoming the person you wish to be. Take control of who you are and consciously decide who you want to become.

Exercise:
Write down three qualities you would wish to radiate into the world. Write down what each of them means to you. Then set out making a daily action with these qualities in mind for 28 days (lunar cycle). For example, if you would like to become more generous, you can leave a 10¢ coin on a wall every day for 28 days for someone else to find. It will only cost you $2.40, but it will bring into your energy

field the precious energy and awareness associated with generosity. If you do this exercise, do not wait to see who picks up the coin. The important fact is that you have left it there, regardless of who benefits from it.

8. UNITY
Earth below, Water above

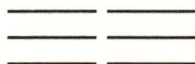

W hen two people enter into a relationship—whether romantic or otherwise—an energy field forms between them and becomes activated whenever they come together, or even when they think of each other at a distance. This field contains their entire history and with each new encounter it is added to and grows. Conversely, once the two people stop seeing each other, stop having feelings for each other, stop speaking to each other, and thinking about each other, the energy field between them begins to dissipate and wither.

There are as many types of energy fields that form up between people as there are people. In fact, there are many more, because each person forms multiple energy fields with different people. An energy field can be toxic or enhancing—it all depends on the investment each person brings to the relationship. The investment can take the form of time spent thinking of each other, the quality of the feelings both parties have for each other, and the actions they take, either in support of or to the detriment of each other.

Unless we live in seclusion, other people will always be part of our life. Our relationships with them can either be energizing, providing us with wellbeing and positive energy, or draining, which happens when we contribute more energy to the relationship field than we receive from it.

It is wise to recognize which relationships will support our life and which will not. Throughout our life's journey we will outgrow many relationships, as friends, acquaintances, colleagues and relatives come and go. Some will remain for as long as we or they are alive, like the relationships with our parents, siblings or spouse. Others will be fleeting encounters, perhaps just a short conversation or a holiday romance. But always there is something to learn from each person we meet and each exchange. Other people are like mirrors that reflect us back to ourselves—how they treat us, what they say to us and the energy they convey are all indicators as to how we appear to them. A wise person cultivates relationships that bring fresh energy into their life and avoids relationships where the demands for energy exceed the supply contributed by the other person. (The exception is the person who deliberately sets out to help another as they go through a difficult time, or the person who becomes a care-giver, looking after the sick or the elderly.)

The people in our life either contribute to our energy intake and process in a positive way or take away from it. We, too, can be an enhancement to another person's life journey or a burden. It is useful to rethink from time to time about one's relationships, especially those that take up most of our time. Are they productive? Do they bring results? If so, what kind of results? Material, emotional, creative, inspirational?

This hexagram is suggesting to re-examine one's relationships in the light of one's future, goals and life commitments. It is a recommendation to invest in relationships that bring positive energy into our life and to disassociate ourselves from energies that are corrosive and harmful.

The Oracle says:
Do you know who your true friends are? If you do, look after them and cherish them because a real friend is a treasure indeed. Within your relationships is the potential for mutual growth, enhancement and wellbeing. Be careful who you mix with and choose your friends carefully.

Exercise:
Make a list of people you feel are your "soul tribe." These are people who inspire you, with whom you feel at ease, even after years of

absence. Once you have your list, refer to it to identify the people who deserve your time and energy, and will most probably always be there for you in your hour of need. Send them good energy and you will be rewarded when they think of you and send vibrant energy back to you.

9. SMALL ACCUMULATION
Heaven below, Wind above

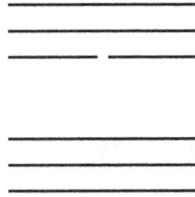

Throughout childhood the energy field or aura surrounding a person acquires form and content. Within this energy field is recorded every moment, every memory, every thought, feeling and action that a person experiences and participates in. It is a recorded history of our life as we experience it and as it unfolds.

The field becomes formed and defined as a person grows up and becomes an adult. According to tradition the aura is fully formed around the age of 21, when one receives the "key to the door." This is the small accumulation of the *I Ching*. More experiences and energy deposits will follow throughout the next 21 years, when the greater accumulation will take place. The small accumulation is our starter pack—the basic faculties, beliefs and energy systems that allow us to successfully navigate through life.

Taking on life is no small task—there is so much to learn, to conquer, to understand. Life is like a wild beast, waiting to be tamed, though few ever really manage to domesticate it, even if they think they have. Inevitably, most people will learn that they have not. There are too many variables, unknowns, unforeseen circumstances to ever really be in control. So best to acknowledge the fact and decide to cooperate with the great forces that govern our destinies.

This is why it is so important to petition, rather than command, and to try and find out what is that special path that is unique to each person on Earth. When on the path and following its course, everything feels right, on time and in harmony, as it should be. When departed from the path, there is chaos, doubt and discord.

Every feeling and every occurence is an indicator and a signpost: Does it feel right? Is it progressive or is it blocking my next step? Are you in the right place and are you on time? Or is there some small adjustment or correction that needs to be made?

We are coming from somewhere and going somewhere. Every moment we are in the narrow part of the hourglass where the shifting sands of time are transmigrating from the future to the past. Every moment counts, as the small accumulation we already have is added to, one grain at a time. As we live our multiple nows we are writing our history. This moment is our time. The future is unknown; the past is already accomplished. But the now is the forge where we temper our destiny and form our story. It is our workshop and our laboratory where we learn about who we are, moderate our behavior and develop winning (or losing) ways.

Everything around us—people, nature, places and circumstances—can be a backdrop to our life's adventure. We can find enhancement in every situation; it depends upon our attitude and mindset. Make this moment count and you will reap its rewards in the future.

This hexagram suggests to add up the value of what you have accumulated so far—the many gifts you have already received. Your experiences, relationships and memories are your treasures that no one can ever take away from you. You have your skills and all the many activities you have learned to master throughout your life so far. You also have your thoughts, your feelings and your ability to act. This is your small accumulation, which is forever growing into your greater accumulation, as the future draws nearer every moment of every day.

The Oracle says:
Learn to read the signs—everything in your life is telling a story. Observe nature and the people around you—are there conflicts or is there harmony? Is communication difficult or easy? Perhaps a small adjustment is needed—look out for new opportunities.

Exercise
Add up the value of your past achievements and successes. Write a
list and look at it often.

Imagine a treasure chest with all your special moments from
the past. At any time, when you feel you need an energy boost, you
can open the chest, pull out one of the gems that have been lodged
inside, polish it up and remind yourself of your moments of glory.

10. CONDUCT
Lake below, Heaven above

Circumstances come and go; prosperity might be elusive or an everyday experience; relationships begin and end. How we conduct ourselves within the many experiences we encounter will determine how happy we can be. Jacques Luceryan in his book *Let There Be Light* wrote that even though he was blind and imprisoned in a World War Two Nazi concentration camp, at no time did he not feel joy. His joy derived from his ability to help others. Jacques knew German and was able to listen in on news broadcasts from the Reich that the camp commanders were listening to, and then report to fellow inmates, passing on to them details about the progress of the Allied front.

Joy and happiness are available at all times. This is an important notion that can help in any situation. The word *conduct*, as in the word *conductor*, describes the flow of electricity and energy. Every person on Earth is a conductor of energy. Our inner well-being depends on the level of electricity or power we conduct.

We conduct energy according to the level of energy we are able to connect to. Our thoughts are our antennae that connect to whatever it is we think about. That is why many sages, thinkers and profits have declared over the centuries that, "You become what you think about." Thoughts consequently lead to actions and feelings. So our life is shaped to a large extent by our ability to think, to plan, to project and to meditate.

Most people are more in control of their lives than they realize. What they think about connects them to energy, which can either sustain them and feed them, or weaken them and make them feel ill. At any given moment we can either be grateful for the gifts we have received in our life, including life itself, or worry about what has not happened, or what we have not been able to accomplish.

From the moment we wake up to the moment we go to bed, we are processing energy. What level of energy we connect to throughout the day is determined by our ability or lack of ability to lift ourselves into the higher energy realms of the planet, that are always available. If conducting finer and higher energies is your goal, then learn to reject the lower and have inspirational call-overs, sayings and meditations that will help you always "look on the bright side of life."

When you think about another person you connect to that person's energy, independent of whether they are far or near; if you think about a past event, you connect to the energy that was present during that event. Therefore, it is important to be discerning what level of energy you will allow into your energy field.

This hexagram suggests it is a wise person who deliberately decides what they will think about and is able to control their emotions. It is an invitation to refine one's intake of energy by thinking in a positive way about the three major influences in our life: the past, the present and the future.

The past has been completed and sealed—we cannot change it; however, we can change how we think about it. Whatever happened in the past, we can always be grateful for lessons learned and experiences we have lived through. The future has not happened yet—it, too, is sealed, waiting for the time when it becomes our present.

The only time we have within which to conduct energies that are as high and powerful as we are able to reach for is the present. That is the power of now.

The Oracle says:
It is a wise person who knows what they think about and is able to control their emotions. Be careful what energy you bring into your aura by how you think, feel and act.

You become what you think about.

Exercise:
Make a list of what you will allow yourself to have emotions about and what you no longer wish to permit yourself to become upset about. Consider including in your list small issues that will no longer matter within a week or two, a month or two, or even a year or two.

11. PEACE
Heaven below, Earth above

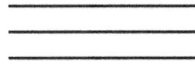

Sometimes in life things become balanced and we are at peace with ourselves and the world. Nothing is missing, and there is no pain. It is a moment in time and surely it will not last. It is important to recognize these moments of peace and harmony, and to be grateful for them while they last, because they will always give way to the next urgency, the next expectancy, the next longing. But peace is always there, forever faithful, waiting to be invited back into our busy lives.

Peace has many faces, but rather than being the absence of stress or conflict, look upon it as the presence of the fullness of the moment and the ability to put aside earthly desires and stresses so that there can be a sense of a higher purpose—a sense of heaven appearing here on Earth.

When all is peaceful and going according to plan, we tend to worry that nothing is happening. At these times, remind yourself that change is coming and remember to enjoy these rare moments—don't rush, but let the natural rhythm of the day take over, if only for a brief while.

There is a strong connection between heaven and Earth. Sometimes we are aware that heaven is appearing on Earth more often and in more places than most people realize—there are many clues demonstrating how universal energies manifest on this planet, but sometimes you need to take a deeper look to see it. Mostly we concentrate on the news of the day and are more concerned about what is happening locally within our man-made culture. In the meantime, there are new cosmic energies appearing on our planet at all times—both from the solar system and from the star belts beyond our local neighbors in space. To see universal energies at work, one only has to look at nature—the shape of a flower, a leaf, or the visible spiral around which a tree grows—sacred geometry is everywhere. We are in heaven, but we are also in hell because we are surrounded by unnatural energies and essences that have been manufactured by humans in their pursuit of the fruits of greed or avarice, or any number of mongrel essences that centuries ago became known as vices.

Sacred geometry is a window into heaven. It is all around us. When you look at a rose, a tomato, an apple or a foxglove, you are looking at sacred geometry. When studying the structure of a crystal, one is calling universal energies to Earth. Many sacred buildings in the world were built to reflect and absorb universal energies, and some were constructed to reflect an image of a star constellation, like Notre Dame in Paris (Virgo) or the great Pyramids in Egypt (Orion).

This mirroring also occurs within the natural worlds on the microscopic level, with atoms resembling solar systems and molecules being akin to entire galaxies.

Crystals are formed around geometric shapes, which reflect sacred geometry. An emerald, for example, is formed around a perfect Seal of Solomon, whereas a salt crystal molecule is a perfect cube.

Our bodies are also diagrams that are designed to process fine and exquisite energies, but it is our choice to train them to do so, if we so desire. For example, five fingers on each hand, five toes on each foot, five holes in the front of our face, a trunk with five extremities (two arms, two legs and a head) indicate the importance of the number five in human affairs. Therefore, in studying the number five and observing it in nature, we can connect to its frequency and learn to appreciate how many flowers, vegetables and plants are tuned to the number five.

When we connect to these heavenly energies and contemplate the way heaven manifests on Earth in the form of sacred geometry, we are able to feel the peace that is a universal property and a gifting from heaven to Earth.

Contemplating the appearance of heaven on Earth, whether in shape, color, number, or in a human act of compassion or generosity, can bring a sense of peace and healing, a moment of settlement that all is well.

Peace can always be found in sleep. We trust sleep and the fact that we will wake up refreshed and ready for a new day. Sleep is a great healer and allows for the comforting passage of time. A new day often brings with it a new perspective and a new opportunity. That is why it is often best to "sleep on it" before making important decisions or taking on a new course of action. It is an opportunity for us to connect to our higher, subconscious selves, where the answers to many of our life dilemmas can be found.

This hexagram suggests you take a moment in your busy day to connect to nature and contemplate the beauty of the natural world. Your body, brain and soul are part of nature and when connected to the natural grid of energies, they will bring you peace and resolution to the many issues you encounter daily.

The Oracle says:
Peace is within you and without you. Heaven on Earth is all around you. Open your eyes to planetary beauty and the harmony of the natural worlds. It is important to sometimes experience peace and to have its balming energy bless your energy field. Develop a value for peace and the ability to invite it into your aura. Learn to be at peace with yourself and your environment.

Exercise:
Imagine you are walking in a beautiful natural landscape. You can feel the warmth of the sun on your skin and you can hear the chirping of the birds, as well as the sound of running water—perhaps a stream or a waterfall—close by. Imagine that you are surrounded by a very light, transparent blue mist. Imagine that this mist is peace and it has come to dwell with you.

I Change

You can use this visualization any time you feel stressed, harassed, and simply need some quiet time to rebalance, resettle and find your inner peace.

12. STAGNATION
Earth below, Heaven above

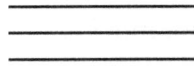

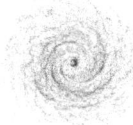

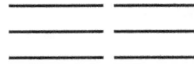

As opposed to peace, with stagnation there is always a sense of something missing. Heaven seems far away and difficult to attain. If peace prevails for too long, it can mean that the natural flow of life has come to a standstill. There is a subtle difference between peace and stagnation, and sometimes the border between them is blurred and it is difficult to ascertain where one ends and the other starts. Peace is a time to gather one's strengths and prepare for re-engagement, whereas stagnation is a time when inactivity begins to drain away one's energy and resources.

Stagnation is a time to strengthen foundations and look to one's fundamentals. The becalming of the sea around us could mean that we have entered the doldrums of life, but that could be the best opportunity to repair sails and check on provisions, looking to the wellbeing of the crew, and making sure that our ship is on course. It is a known fact that when sailing toward a destination, the boat or ship is not on course most of the time; it continuously needs to correct course as it drifts once to one side of the course, and then to the other.

Times of stagnation are not really stagnant at all; they are moments of pause—time to regroup and restate one's purpose. This is a time to consider the great issues of life and look to nature and the heavens for inspiration.

When we look at the stars at night, we might feel a sense of longing. Nothing is perfect on Earth and we will always aim for perfection, or if not perfection, then for improvement and something better. Longing is a natural human emotion because as long as we live on planet Earth, we are struggling for continuance in an imperfect world.

It is natural for humans to dream. Sometimes it feels like we are not moving forward in the direction of our dreams. The way out of stagnation is to take action. Sometimes any action will do to get the ship moving again, as long as that action is motivated by our goals.

This hexagram has two aspects. On the one hand it suggests spending time in nature, appreciating the richness and variety that Mother Earth offers to our senses every moment of every day. But it is also a time to look to one's next steps or resolutions that can bring one out of stagnation into the flow of one's life. It encourages us to find an action that will inspire us to progress to the next stage of our development.

The Oracle says:
Take a moment to consider your journey so far and where you would want to go. One action a day can bring you out of the standstill onto the open road where opportunity abounds.

Exercise:
Consider a goal you would like to achieve in life. Then imagine that attaining that goal is a journey. Next, design seven stations along that journey and give them names—seven stages on the way to your dream. For example, if your plan is to write a book, the seven stations might be—

1. Define 12 chapter titles
2. Write an outline
3. Write the first three chapters
4. Write the next three chapters
5. Write the next three chapters
6. Write the next three chapters
7. Get it published.

13. COMMUNITY
Fire below, Heaven above

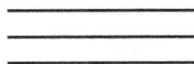

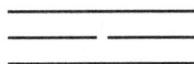

Most of us cannot survive on our own. It is true that there are people who choose to live in seclusion and thrive in their solitude. In past ages there have been religious sects whose members, like the anchorites, would wall themselves in or live in a cave for years at a time.

In her book *Cave in the Snow*, Vicki Mackenzie writes about Tenzin Palmo, a British born Tibetan nun, and her twelve year journey into solitude and meditation. After years of seclusion, three of which were spent in complete isolation, Tenzin, whose name at birth was Diane Perry, emerged from her austere existence to become an ambassador for Tibetan Buddhism, traveling the world, lecturing and fund raising to establish a Buddhist nunnery for girls who previously had had very limited access to education and the study of traditional scripture. In her years of living in the Himalaya Mountains she understood that she had a mission to fulfill and now she is spreading her message. She has taken on the task of establishing equal rights and opportunities for learning for her charges.*

Most of us have a mission or a calling that involves other people. We derive satisfaction from helping, teaching or sharing with others and we crave recognition and appreciation. Fame is a big lure, especially to the young, because once a person establishes a fan base, however large or small, one can draw on the energies of people who admire you, as the fans send their energies to the object of their

---

* *Check out the documentary movie about Tenzin Palmo, titled, like the book about her,* Cave in the Snow.

admiration. However, dependence on the opinions and admiration of other people can also lead to one's downfall, because adoring fans mostly send their idol a very low-grade energy, which can cause excitement and boost one's ego in the short run, but will hold the person back from their natural evolutionary path in the long term, because mostly fans want their idol to remain exactly as they are. Energies from admirers are usually accompanied by demands and requirements. For example, if we like a particular performer, we want them to produce more of the kind of music we like to hear.

A wise person will strive for self-respect before they expect or demand respect from others; they will not depend on others for their daily energy feed or expect to become famous without becoming a master of their craft, whatever that craft happens to be.

As we mature, grow and develop, our group of friends will change and evolve with us. It is essential to value the people in our lives who provide companionship and support on a daily basis, especially those who ask for or demand nothing. To process higher energies, it is essential to reciprocate the good will of others and pay it forward, so that we become more of a giver than a taker.

This hexagram indicates the importance of community and friends. It suggests that one should appreciate the friends and colleagues one already has as well as the need to cultivate new ones.

The Oracle says:
Rather than hoping for fans, a wise person will cultivate a community of like-minded people, with whom he or she can exchange ideas, hopes and plans. These will be people who can offer constructive criticism without bias and be a support system in times of hardship and need.

Exercise:
Write down the names of five friends, then next to their names, write down their qualities that you like and admire. What do these friends say about you? You are like your friends in many ways. Do you have the qualities you admire in your friends? Do your friends provide

good energy, and do you reciprocate the same? Or do they (or some of them) drain you of energy? If so, perhaps you should reconsider who you wish to be friends with.

14. POSSESSIONS
Heaven below, Fire above

Depending upon who you are and how wealthy you are, you probably have fewer or more possessions (there could be exceptions to this rule, like a very rich person who has very little, or a poor person with lots of junk). Some possessions support us in our maintenance, like our homes, kitchen utensils, or warm clothing; some we become attached to, like souvenirs, photographs or favorite pieces of art; and some are part of the scenery, like a rug, a shower curtain, or a bedspread.

Some possessions carry an energetic charge for us, if each time we look at them we feel enhanced and pleased. Others can have an opposite effect, if they are reminders of times we would prefer to forget, or if they no longer fit into our current life, like love letters from an affair which had ended long ago. Sometimes we hang onto possessions because someone we like, value or feel obliged to has given them to us. Possessions can be liked or disliked, valued or not valued, appreciated or ignored.

The danger occurs when we believe that our possessions define who we are. It is important to remember that we will not be taking any of our possessions with us when we go and that all the things we possess will be distributed to our heirs, and will consequently be discarded or sold.

In the documentary film *The Flat*, the filmmaker Amon Goldfinger and his family go through his grandmother's effects after her death. The objects in the apartment are mostly reminders of old times when, for example, women wore fox fur stoles with the head and feet still attached, or when they had multiple pairs of gloves to go with their various outfits. When he finds a medal with a Nazi emblem on one side and the Seal of Solomon on the other, this leads to a whole investigation which is the main theme of the film. Most of his mother's possessions are soon disposed of as bags of trash, as the family prepares to sell the apartment. It is amazing how many things the deceased woman, Gerda Tuchler, had accumulated over the 70 years she had lived in the flat, after having fled from Nazi Germany in the 1930s.

We all have possessions, whether many or few. How many of our possessions are useful and used on a daily, weekly, monthly or seasonal basis? How many are there for decoration and to make life easier and/or more pleasant? How many are forgotten, hidden away in drawers, or gathering dust at the back of shelves or on closet floors?

This hexagon says that perhaps it is time to review one's possessions and to take a good look at all the things you have accumulated through the years. How important are they? And if they are, perhaps it is time to attach to them renewed value and appreciation. If not, perhaps it is time to discard those possessions that no longer carry with them a valid reason for being there.

The Oracle says:
Make sure your possessions do not possess you. Cherish your possessions and look after them, but realize that, just like your body, they are on lease and you will possess them for a brief period only. You cannot possess this moment because in a moment it will be confined to history and become yet another memory, to add to your increasing collection of memories. Free yourself from unnecessary possessions.

Exercise:
Make a list of your most precious possessions. What would you do if you lost them? Realize that nothing is irreplaceable because even an old photograph or letter from a loved one can be recreated in memory or replaced by a live encounter.

15. MODESTY
Mountain below, Earth above

I n today's day and age modesty does not mean what it used to in, say, Victorian times, when women wore long dresses, hats and gloves, and there were definite rules governing the chaperoned interaction between men and women prior to their commitment to exchange marital vows.

Modesty is not a word that is often heard these days, following the sexual revolution of the 60s and the explicit language and behavior exhibited by pop stars, entertainers and artists of various ilks.

Modesty has nothing to do with covering up body parts, though the essence of modesty might cause a person to do so. A modest person does not accept praise when they feel that praise is not earned; they know their worth enough to not need to proclaim it from the rooftops.

There is a natural modesty that is the opposite to exhibitionism, boasting or self-glorification. Our victories are seen; we do not have to proclaim them to the whole world for them to be appreciated and noticed. All of our achievements and experiences are lodged inside our energy field in the form of electrical impulses and signals. That is why clairvoyants and energetically sensitive people can read our history as well as our character traits that are our strengths which can contribute to our future success.

Real modesty stems from the recognition that we humans have a special place in creation, but it also means that we do not usurp a position beyond our station. Someone who thinks they can dictate to others what they can or cannot do, think or believe, is not modest. They are bullies, dictators and autocrats. A modest person gives another the space to be themselves, to make their own mistakes, and to discover for themselves who they are and what they are here on Earth to do and accomplish.

This hexagram suggests there might be an area of your life in which you are being less than modest. It might be time to review whether you are not attempting to influence another person's decisions without giving them enough room to think and act for themselves. Are you being judgmental about the behavior of others? Realize that you never have the full picture when you assess another person's decisions, and you probably do not know their thinking process that has led them to do what they do.

The Oracle says:
As your life moves from the past, through the present into the future, write and build the best life story you can—it is you responsibility to construct a unique narrative that others can value and appreciate, if it is indeed worthy of value and appreciation.

Exercise:
Learn to accept compliments for what they are. Next time someone praises you and you feel the praise has been earned, accept it with grace and poise. Otherwise, if you deny the compliment, you are rejecting the energy that has been offered to you. If, on the contrary, you ask for more, by saying, for example, "Do you really think so?" you are "tugging"—trying to solicit additional energy from the person who has just paid you a compliment.

16. ENTHUSIASM
Earth below, Thunder above

Enthusiasm is a quality that opens up the pathway to the spirit. It allows a person to overcome difficulties and obstacles, and to achieve their goals. A person who is enthusiastic about a project or a tasking is less likely to quit or become disappointed, than a person who is not. Enthusiasm brings with it extra energy and an enlarged vision which allows a person to see the way ahead more clearly.

Aligning one's life to one's enthusiasm is easier than attempting to align one's enthusiasm to one's life. So how can this be done? Enthusiasm lives in the vicinity of actions and endeavors that one loves. The more we are able to bring these into our lives and maintain them, the more enthusiasm will join us on our journey through time.

Where does enthusiasm come from? When does it appear? Enthusiasm is often the result of the coming together of an internal projection or goal and a perceived clearing of the road ahead. It is when you know what you are doing and why you are doing it; it is in the joining with other people or energies that allow you to become active and effective on your chosen path.

Enthusiasm is a natural human property. It accompanies us throughout our life when we are at peace with ourselves and in harmony with our surroundings. Only then can a drop of this sacred substance find us, adding significance and importance to our decisions and actions.

Enthusiasm can be manufactured from the inside or connected to from the outside. It will manifest from the inside every time you engage in an activity or with a person you are enthusiastic about. You can connect to it from the outside when you are in company with someone or some people who are enthusiastic about what they are doing.

Enthusiasm is contagious. You can also catch the way of it from someone who is enthusiastic by nature. It can spread through an audience listening to a speaker, or jump from person to person. It adds brightness and enjoyment to any gathering.

The Oracle says:
Keep your enthusiasm close by so you can dip into it, like into a bank account, when you feel your energy of determination is running low.

Exercise:
Try to connect to enthusiasm when you are not feeling particularly enthusiastic. Find an activity you enjoy and make time to practice it on a regular basis.

17. ADAPTING TO THE TIMES
Thunder below, Lake above

Our life is changing all the time and we are changing, too, learning to adapt to new situations, new requirements, new fashions, and new relationships.

The lake might appear calm, but there is the influence of thunder underneath. Change is always accompanying us, even when we feel that nothing is happening. A wise person knows this and takes advantage of the quiet times—putting their house in order and getting ready for the next upheaval, which will inevitably come. So rather than becoming frustrated or bored, they will use the time wisely, settling unfinished business and tidying their affairs.

In our lives we have times when we become leaders of self and times when we appear to be followers, simply because there is no need at the time to assert ourselves or lead by example. Thus our portrayal and behavior become more serene, even though the thunder awaits within the depths of the lake. In our relationships sometimes we are leaders and sometimes we are followers. A teacher might be a leader to his students, but himself he is a student when it comes to honing his craft and developing his skills.

There is no point in resisting the changing seasons, for winter comes, whether we like it or not. A wise person embraces the changes in their life and is grateful for what they have achieved so far, knowing that they still have time to add to their experience and education in a way that will help them become wiser, stronger and better. As Shakespeare wisely pointed out—when winter comes, can spring be far behind?

In the energy worlds all humans develop a following. Like

goes to like and according to what we think, do and radiate, so will we attract the energies that recognize their own. Thus observe what and who is attracted to you because that will give you a reading of who you are at this time, bearing in mind that you can decide to change and that life is cyclical, with highs and lows, and times of apparent calm.

We are all followers as well as having an energetic following, but the question arises—what or whom do we follow? If we make the decision to always follow the truth, then ours will be a path of learning and development, within which we can wake up each morning with a clear conscience, ready to face a new beginning of a new day.

So we can decide who or what we wish to follow. Some people are the followers of fashion, which is a skin deep manifestation of current trends; others are followers of more permanent qualities, like patience or learning. The choice is yours.

Following denotes a sequence in time and space. We always follow those who have come before us and precede those who will come after us. The question is, can we learn from those who preceded us and be a good example to those who follow?

Followers are also leaders, and leaders are also followers—thus the eternal dance between the two. In a dance, the man leads and the woman follows, but you could also say that the fact of needing to lead causes the man to become a follower of his partner and her needs. Thus the teacher learns from the student and the sage from the acolyte, just as much as the student learns from the teacher and the acolyte from the sage.

This hexagon says that although the image of a follower might appear to be of someone in a passive stance, you can take the initiative and deliberately make the decision to follow who or what you want to invite into your life.

The Oracle says:
To follow says to come after or later. We are born at a time that follows many golden ages which have produced

many great thinkers and doers—both men and women. We can follow in their footsteps and learn from their example.

Exercise:
Make a decision what or who you want to follow. Then take deliberate actions to connect to those people or those energies so they may play a greater part in your life. Find out more about them by researching their lives and works.

18. DECAY
Wind below, Mountain above

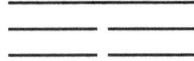

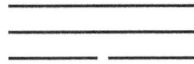

Decay is a natural process. Everything that exists in the material worlds—the moment it is created, it begins its journey toward its demise. Even the pyramids will eventually turn back to dust, whether it takes thousands or even millions of years.

Natural growth in the organic worlds of fauna, flora and humans follows a path of development. The human story begins with growth from a baby to adulthood; a plant grows from seed to a mature bloom, and an animal grows from cub to bear, from duckling to duck, and so on. Then decay of the material host sets in and a person or animal grows older and loses their vigor of youth. Timelines vary, as a human lives longer than their pet, and an elephant lives longer than a human, but everything that is born must die. It is a law; you could say that birth is also a death sentence.

As opposed to the material worlds, the energy worlds obey a completely different law. Once created, energy cannot be destroyed. Since we are part flesh and part energy, there is that part of us that cannot be destroyed, does not decay, and will survive the death of the physical body.

All the energies we connect to, process, and release from ourselves will continue to exist, perhaps in a different form, but adding to the energy realms of planet Earth nevertheless. Our anger, fears, hopes, desires as well as such qualities as love, compassion, peace or generosity are all everlasting commodities and will survive us and continue to exist long after we will have passed away and ventured upon our next journey, whatever that turns out to be.

When we die we will take with us the qualities we grow and nourish in our lifetime which become part of our radiating life. We will then wish we had more of those sacred substances, so a wise person deliberately sets out to collect these higher qualities which can become their passport to their next incarnation.

This hexagon talks about the transmuting of energies. A plant, a tree, or an animal is dedicated to a specific frequency, which is constant and unchanging from day to day or year to year. But a human can choose what he wants to connect to and can then set about realizing his goals.

The Oracle says:
When you encounter a lower energy or a messy situation, realize that you can successfully set about cleaning it up and putting something better in its place.

Exercise:
Next time you are in a situation where you feel that someone else's energy is dragging you down—perhaps because they are depressed or full of complaint—make an effort to lift them up by introducing a happy thought or inspiring subject to talk about.

19. APPROACH
Lake below, Earth above

Beginnings and endings are important because they set the tone for what is then to follow. Both beginnings and endings are really beginnings because as one stage of the journey ends, another one begins. By the same token, you could say that both beginnings and endings are really endings, because as one stage of the journey begins, another one ends. As you say goodbye to a loved one, you are starting a period of separation, however long it might turn out to be. How you say your goodbyes and what kind of sentiment accompanies the farewell will set the tone for this next stage in your relationship.

People form an opinion of us within the first few seconds of meeting us, even before a word is said or a hand is shaken. Then everything that follows will either confirm those first impressions or contradict them, so that the person we meet will either feel that they had assessed us correctly from the start, or they will feel they have to take another look and reassess their snap judgment.

When you meet a successful person, you will no doubt be impressed by the way they greet you, the way they introduce themselves and the way they assert themselves. How we think of ourselves radiates through our every gesture, action and utterances. A great actor enters the stage, and even before he or she says anything, they bring with them an aura and a presence that is undeniable. It is those first moments that set the scene and establishes a person's sense of command.

When you enter a room, you bring with you your energy and all those qualities, essences and forces that attend you. You also bring your experiences and skills, all of which can contribute to your success, or undermine your belief in yourself. To be effective in your beginnings, bring to mind the unique energies and attributes that you contribute and how you can improve any situation.

This hexagon advises about new beginnings—perhaps a new job, a new relationship or a new adventure. Whatever it might be, there is a new opportunity opening up, and your attitude will determine whether it will bring success or failure.

The Oracle says:
Know yourself and your best features; believe in yourself
and trust in your ability to succeed.

Exercise
Write down the qualities that are part of your energetic make-up, like, for example, honesty, patience, generosity, or serenity. When meeting new people or entering a new situation, call over these qualities and invite them to assist you in your new venture.

20. OBSERVATION
Earth below, Wind above

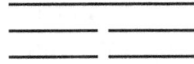

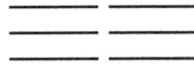

From an energy perspective, the sense of sight is the most powerful of all the senses. The moment we see something, we connect to it energetically and take into ourselves its frequency. Seeing is believing, the old adage says. Once we see something, we own its energy and it is ours to keep.

Being a witness is to participate in an event and to add one's energy to the power the event gathers to itself. That is why important ceremonies and celebrations are always witnessed and shared. How good would a performance be without its spectators? Or a religious mass without a congregation? The most powerful events in world history always involved large numbers of people.

The eyes are linked directly to the brain and whatever they see—the image of it gets directly transmitted to our brains for storage. The eyes say *yes* because even if we disapprove of whatever it is that we are seeing, we are still taking it into ourselves and preserving it for future reference. The brain remembers what it sees, which is why we can recall everything we have experienced under hypnosis, even if personally we do not remember a particular event.

Observation is different from seeing. It involves paying attention and a deliberate involvement in what we are observing. When we see something, we can choose to either mechanically note what we are seeing, or we can observe it. Everything we see can become meaningful, if we choose to contemplate how it changes through time. The moment by moment kaleidoscope of what passes before our eyes, as we go about our day, can provide us with a reading of who we are, how the world responds to us and where we are heading. Who are the people we associate with? Where do we live? How do we spend our time? Where do we work? Our surroundings define us and provide color, background, and flavor to our portrait.

The Earth supports us and the winds of change are constantly blowing into our lives new circumstances, new feelings and new perceptions as we age and grow in experience.

The difference between seeing something and observing it is that seeing is automatic, without engaging a thought process about it. While we are awake we constantly see, whether looking at a computer screen, or walking down a street. We might see something and not even remember we have seen it. Who can remember all the faces they have seen on a busy subway station or in a crowd at a performance, or a football game?

Observation is more deliberate, like a scientist watching an experiment, or a dog breeder looking for the signs which will tell him whether a particular dog is ready to give birth or not. When you observe something, you participate in its energetic process. You become involved and take into yourself more of the energy of what it is you are observing than if you were merely seeing it.

You might be surprised by someone in your circle and how influential they can become in your life, if you pay attention to the signs the universe is sending you.

This hexagon is suggesting we bring our conscious mind into the process of seeing, so we can observe our surroundings and the people we spend time with, whether at work or socially, in a more deliberate manner.

The Oracle says:
Pay attention to the backdrop of your life. It will tell you much about who you are. The quality of the people you mix with, live with and work with will give you an indication as to who you are and the kind of energy you associate with.

Observe only what will serve you. Learn to observe discriminately and with a purpose so that the energy you connect to during your time of observation can contribute to your spiritual journey and enhance your wellbeing.

Exercise

Write a list of your ten favorite movies. Underneath (or next to) each title write down what it is that you like about it. Then try and condense what you have written to a single word or phrase, like adventure, romance, humanity, justice. Once you have your single word, which most probably will be a description of a quality and an energy, make a conscious decision whether you want more of this quality in your life (or not).

21. BITING THROUGH
Thunder below, Fire above

When thunder strikes and the fires are raging, there is only one solution: keep going, because this will eventually pass. These are extreme circumstances. In difficult times it is the core of who we are and what we want that can keep us going and help us retain our sanity.

Thunder is a manifestation of a lightning strike, but it occurs after the lightning had already struck, as it travels at the speed of sound, which is slower than the speed of light. So when you hear thunder, it means the worst is already over. The roll of thunder sounds ominous, but is harmless in itself. However, the fire caused by the lightning can burn and destroy.

When the elements are raging all around you, you hunker down and close the hatches, waiting for it to pass. It is important to have the right supplies and to be prepared for any circumstance that may come your way. However, no matter how difficult your circumstance, as long as you are alive, improvement is possible.

Everything eventually passes, and whatever you are witnessing now, or whatever your current difficulties might be, that will pass also. Any tree you see, any building you visit, or live in, any person you might meet, will no longer be here in 100, 200, 300 or more years in the future. Even the pyramids in Egypt and elsewhere will eventually be gone.

Your life will pass, just like this storm, so make the most of every moment. When there is a temporary drama in your life, you can always look at it from the perspective of 100 years into the future. As you do this, note how your problem quickly reduces in size.

This hexagon reminds you of the temporary nature of life and all material things on Earth. Whatever might be bothering you today will pass, so worry not. Have peace of mind so you can find solutions to any problem or obstacle that might come your way.

The Oracle says:
Look to the bigger picture and see your life as one short step in a whole sequence of lives.

Exercise
If you were to reincarnate back to Earth, where, when, and into what family would you choose to return? Would you prefer to reincarnate backward or forward in time? Would you choose the same family, race, country, or petition for a different kind of experience? You might just get what you ask for!

22. GRACE
Fire below, Mountain above

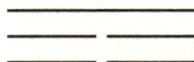

They say punctuality is the courtesy of kings. This does not necessarily mean that a person who is punctual is royal, or that every ruler is punctual. Punctuality is an outward display of refinement, but it can be learned, and does not necessarily reflect a person's respect for other people's time. However, if punctuality comes from an inner appreciation of and respect for time—one's own, and that of others—it becomes a display of a person's inner process and reasoning.

There is a saying, "What is outside is always on the inside, but not everything inside is visible on the outside." In other words, it takes time for qualities and traits to migrate from the inside to the outside. When an actor plays a role or a con man puts on a disguise, their outside becomes a portrayal of someone they are not on the inside. A person can pretend to be caring and empathetic to gain favor with another person, but true altruism and care have a very definite radiation; eventually the imposter will be found out.

So, an outer portrayal of refinement could mean either that the person is indeed refined on the inside as well, or that they have learned how to portray refinement to disguise the lack of refinement inside.

Etiquette and outer refinement can be useful in social circumstances, where norms and conventions can smooth and ease interactions between people, but they do not necessarily indicate inner refinement.

When punctuality comes from a respect for other people's time, as well as your own, the energy of respect will begin to live within your aura. When you realize that being late can cause worry and a waste of time, you will make the effort to be timely and on time. Time is a commodity not to be wasted; arriving late and in a hurry can rob you, as well as the person you are meeting, of your composure and preparedness.

This hexagram warns that outer refinement does not necessarily mean inner refinement. It calls for a closer look—are your relationships based on an outer portrayal or do you look deeper to see what kind of balances, standards and moralities live behind the mask?

The Oracle says:
Everyone you meet has many levels of display and behavior. Learn to ask the questions that will guide you to discover the deeper sentiments of the people you form relationships with.

Exercise
Taking the last week as an example, have you been punctual for the commitments you had made to other people? Think of the meetings, deadlines and dates you had committed to during the last seven days. If you were punctual, why were you? Was it mechanical, because others require it of you, or do you feel a respect for your time and the time of others? Does your behavior reflect inner refinement or is it just skin deep?

22. END OF A RELATIONSHIP
Earth below, Mountain above

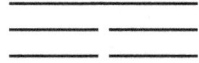

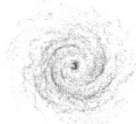

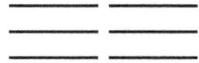

Throughout our lives we make and break off many relationships. At first we establish relationships with our parents, siblings, relatives and friends. We then develop relationships at school, at work and in the place where we live. We are constantly forming and ending relationships, as we finish school or college, begin or change jobs, move away to a new place, start dating and meet the family and friends of our significant other.

We are like a revolving door—meeting, greeting, saying hello and goodbye. People move away, they die, or they simply fade away from our lives as we grow up and develop our ever changing circle of friends and acquaintances.

Sometimes it is hard to say goodbye; sometimes we lose a friend without even the luxury of a farewell. But all relationships here on Earth will eventually end—there is no "forever" or "for eternity." As all who have ever lost a friend or a partner says, remember to enjoy the moments you share and, above all, tell them how you feel.

Sometimes, when a relationship ends, it feels like the end of the world. You might wonder how you will continue to go on. But time is a great healer and the grief will pass and transform into appreciation for the history you have shared together. You still are custodian to your memories and even if the person has gone, you can still connect to their energies and qualities.

This hexagram reminds us that relationships come and go, and that it is important to learn to go with the flow of life, within which every stage has a beginning, middle and end.

The Oracle says:
As one relationship ends, another one begins. The one lasting
relationship you have is the relationship with yourself.

Exercise
Write down the names of five people who form the most important
relationships in your life. Write a letter to each one, describing your
value for them and your appreciation for the qualities and good
times they have shared with you. If you feel it is appropriate, give
them the letter at a time that feels right.

24. RETURN
Wind below, Earth above

I n every life there comes a time for a life review. One of the main times when it seems to come upon us is in our mid-life—a time which some refer to as a crisis, but could also be looked upon as a new opportunity opening up. For most people there are many times when we ask ourselves who we are and where we are going. As in the mid-life years, this is a time when everything comes into question— are we on the right path, should we continue in the same vein, are we surrounded by the right people who love us and support us, or are we missing something? Have we sacrificed what we wanted to achieve in life so that we could survive and look after a family? Are we satisfied or is satisfaction still eluding us? What can we bring back into our life that we used to enjoy but have abandoned out of duty, obligation, responsibility? Can we reconsider the purpose of our life and bring it back on track? Where does service and helping others fit in?

This is a time when we realize for sure that we are not immortal and that the day will inevitably come when we will have to depart from this Earth and enter a new life. At the halfway point time speeds up and urgency sets in. If you go away on a holiday for a week, by the end of day three, thoughts of returning home begin to reappear and concerns about what next needs to be done begin to claim you. The half-way point of a life or a project is no different—the energetic influence arriving from the other end begins to manifest and make itself known.

If you are not yet at your halfway mark, or perhaps well past it, this time of questioning might still apply to you.

Life is full of turning points—from childhood to the teenage years, then taking on responsibility for one's own life and perhaps those of others as well, arriving at the mid-life opportunity, and then facing menopause or what is known as andropause for men, then old age and finally, departure. Each stage of life has its gifts and its requirements. It is important to embrace change as it comes upon us and learn to master the age we are experiencing right now. It will pass as we approach the next age that is waiting in the wings. It is important to gather good memories and experiences to take with us into our next adventure.

This hexagram is an invitation to see your life as a continuum with many different stages. It is like a rainbow journey wherein each age offers different experiences and opportunities. Do not wish you were younger than you are—today is the best age you could possibly be; make the most of it!

The Oracle says:
Slow down and take a good look. Time is speeding up but you need to be in opposition to its bidding. Re-examine all your commitments and everything you are doing on a regular basis. Eliminate what is unimportant so you can concentrate on what is important. What is important? Those activities and initiatives that will help you become what you would want to be in the approaching days, weeks and years.

Exercise
Make a list of what you hope to achieve in this next part of your life—whether one year, three years or a decade. Make a plan to achieve your goals—writing down a series of steps or milestones that can lead you toward your desired result.

25. UNEXPECTED MISFORTUNE
Thunder below, Heaven Above

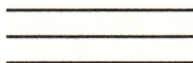

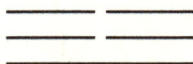

When asked about the meaning of honesty, most people will say that it is about telling the truth and it is the opposite to lying. However, there are many degrees of honesty because a person who does not lie can still be dishonest by concealing or hiding the truth. Complete honesty is full disclosure and complete transparency; it is having nothing to hide and being open, above all to oneself.

Most people do have something in their past that they are not proud of and would prefer not to talk about. How can such a person be honest and decide to rid their life of dishonesty? Honesty can start from now. A person can decide at any point to become honest and to promote honesty as a way of life.

So it is not about admitting past sins or openly declaring all one's secrets. The past can remain in the past. But the energies of the present are alive and influencing us every moment of every day. So it is in the here and now that we can make the decision to be honest, to lead an open life and to become someone who, if we were our friend, we would be proud to associate with.

Honesty to self is based in knowing oneself. Mostly we do not control our emotions, but when they occur and suddenly we feel a wave of, say, anger, or remorse, or gratitude—do we know why? Is it a past experience, a memory, a bias, or perhaps an instinct of self-preservation that causes us to feel what we feel? Or could it be that we are picking up someone else's emotions and letting them play out through our systems? Honesty to self means following up an unexpected emotion with a process of reasoning, to detect and decode the source of the feeling in order to take one step closer toward the ability to control our emotions and actions.

One of the hallmarks of an honest person is the ability to laugh at oneself. A comedian can see the dishonesty of people around him or her as funny, and knows how to create amusing images and revealing understandings from their experiences in everyday life. We can become a comedian to ourselves, seeing our own experiences as funny, rather than embarassing.

This hexagram warns of an unexpected event that can bring up spontaneous emotions—stimulated from the outside. Try to identify these emotions by giving them names—say, jealousy, regret, or envy—because once you have their names, you can learn to master them and cut short the time they might take control over you.

The Oracle says:
You can substitute lower emotions with higher feelings, like substituting compassion for judgement, tolerance for bigotry, generosity for jealousy, patience for impatience, or love for hate.

Exercise
Next time you feel a lower emotion taking over, spend a few minutes trying to understand why you are feeling this way. Write down the source of your emotion and contemplate its opposite, which can neutralize and heal.

26. CULTIVATION
Heaven below, Mountain above

Sometimes everything goes well in life and we have a success in our work or meet a person who we think might become our life partner. Sometimes others will appreciate us for who we are and we feel that life is on the right track. This is the time to practice restraint and not become complacent, because everything can change in the blink of an eye. This is the time to be grateful for any success you might have enjoyed, and to increase your efforts to keep the positive results coming. Life is full of surprises and it will always test us, but each test is an obstacle to overcome. Even the good times will end, but life will continue and it is important to always be equal to the challenge, whatever that challenge might be— the good, the bad and the ugly.

To be born on planet Earth is a very special privilege—you are one in many millions who are alive at this time of transition from the age of Pisces into the age of Aquarius. Perhaps you were sent here on a very special mission and you are just beginning to understand what that mission is.

The Dagara tribe in Africa have a ceremony during which they ask an unborn child why it has come to their village and how can the elders help it fulfill its destiny. For this purpose they put the pregnant mother into a trance and ask her to be the child's mouth-piece.

If you were a member of the Dagara tribe, do you know what your mother would have told the tribal elders? And if you think you do know, what kind of help would she have asked for in fulfilling your life's mission? We are here on Earth at this time for a reason, but we do not always know what that reason is. It can take a lifetime to find out what it is, but if we are open to being responsive to our mission, it might reveal itself sooner rather than later.

This hexagram is telling you to be grateful for what you have and to never underestimate the gifts you have been given, both at birth and later in life as you were growing up and learning about the place where you live and the people who have come into your life. This hexagram is suggesting that you find ways to teach, to help and to share your experiences.

The Oracle says:
While you are here in life, you have the unique ability to learn, to grow and to have the opportunity to reincarnate, whether here on Earth or elsewhere in Creation.

Exercise
Write down all the gifts you had received at birth—life itself, your body, your senses, your family, your environment. Call over often that this is a grant from Creation and that you have the responsibility to pay back for your existence by wisely using the gifts entrusted to you.

27. NOURISHMENT
Thunder below, Mountain above

Everything that is alive needs nourishment. Plants and trees need to process water, minerals from the earth and sunlight to grow. Humans need five kinds of food: physical food, liquid, air, energy and light. Each food is digested by our systems and transformed into body building blocks, fat and energy.

We receive energy not only from the food we eat, but also from the sun, the universe and from our thoughts and emotions. Both thoughts and emotions can drain us of energy or help connect us to a higher source of energy.

Have you ever felt upset or angry and consequently felt drained, tired or even exhausted (the state of exhaustion meaning that there is not a supply of energy left to call upon in one's hour of need)? Where and who do we get our nourishment from will determine the level of energy we are able to connect to.

Some people believe that surrounding oneself with fine art and beautiful things will bring into one's energy field sublime essences that had inspired those works of art in the first place. The pictures one hangs on one's wall as well as the photographs one displays in one's home will be reminders of happy moments, and cherished relationships. By looking at a picture, one can connect to the energy of another person and feel their presence. It is like dialing their number on the telephone—their image connects to their frequency, wherever in the world they might be.

Nourishment can also come from the language one uses. Every word is a container of energy and can be used as a means of connection to an object (noun), an action (verb), or a feeling. When you describe a scene or an event from the past, you reconnect to the energies that were present when that event had taken place. It also allows you to convey what it felt like to be present at that moment in time, so your listener can benefit from your experience and participate in your life by sharing your experiences.

There are two aspects to the nourishment you ingest and express, both of which relate to your mouth. One is concerned with the physical food and liquids you take into yourself on a daily basis, and the other is to do with the language that comes out of your mouth. Both can be refined; the more you develop and become sensitive, the more you need to pay attention to the words that escape your lips and the foods you eat.

This hexagram suggests you pay attention to the foods you eat, the liquids you drink, the air you breathe, and the energies you take into yourself. Your health and progress depends not only upon what goes into your mouth and nose, but what comes out of your mouth in the form of words, sentences and levels of speech. This hexagram also suggests you never cease to improve your vocabulary and express positive thoughts and emotions by how you describe them in words.

The Oracle says:
What comes out of your mouth in speech is more connective to the energy worlds than the food you eat. Jesus, the teacher from Galilee rightly says, "A man is not defiled by what enters his mouth, but by what comes out of it." (Matthew 15, 11)

Exercise
Spend a day not saying the word "I." See how easy or difficult it is to do. Realize that when you say "I," you are using high octane energy fuel, connecting to the core of your being. By becoming more aware of your usage of language, you will increase your sensitivity to the potential your words offer you as a means of connection to higher energies.

28. EXCESS
Wind below, Lake above

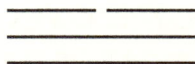

This hexagram speaks of abundance. Abundance can go two ways—it can be too much or it can be the fulfillment of one's desires. Sometimes a person can win the lottery or come into a large inheritance; if they are not prepared for it, they can then spend it all and lose more of what they already had. Having money is a skill and not many people know how to acquire it. That is why not many people are rich.

An excess of energy can have a similar result. If, for example, a person becomes an overnight success, they will receive masses of energy from their fans and from people who are thinking of them, perhaps envying them, and wondering about their success. That is a lot of energy to handle, especially for a young person who is not prepared for such adulation. Often pop stars who do become an overnight success turn to drugs and/or alcohol to cope with their newfound fame and the pressures exerted by managers, agents, groupies and fans. There should be a school for fame where budding artists are taught how to handle the onslaught public recognition—the hot energy that seeks to invade one's space and claim any bit of gossip, information or image to feed the craze.

Wealth and fame can be dangerous, but in the hands of a person who has determination and a sense of purpose, these two energetic sisters can be managed and kept at bay. The important ingredient is to maintain a private life and not end up depending on the whim of the crowds, because fans can be fickle. They can be adoring one day and bored with the person and their style the next. So whatever the excess you encounter in your life, treat it as a

I Change

transient appearance—here today, gone tomorrow.

To connect to excess in terms of energy, it is important to have a clear vision and a definite goal or purpose.

This hexagram suggests that great achievements are possible for someone with a singular vision and powerful determination. There is no shortage of energy in the world, and no shortage of resources necessary to build a career or achieve one's dreams. The skill is to arrange one's life to a purpose, by directing more energy toward oneself. One way to think of this is that energy is a river and when we truly desire something, we can build a dam and direct extra energy into our reservoir, which in turn feeds into our desired outcome. Know what you want and call over the image of what you want to achieve often. By feeding your vision you will bring it closer to yourself.

The Oracle says:
Before you can achieve your desires you need to be specific in describing what you want.

Exercise
Create a vision board—a collage of pictures and words representing what you desire. Look at it often and imagine what it will feel like when the various goals comes to pass.

I Change

29. THE ABYSS
Water below, Water above

Water is on the one hand unpredictable, and on the other it is dependable. Always adapting to its container, it is also in constant flux, changing with the weather, the temperature, the season and the tidal pull of the moon.

We consist mostly of water, so at a physical level we too are subject to fluctuations. This can be seen, for example, in the emotional ups and downs a woman goes through during her monthly cycle.

There are three forms of water—ice, which is fixed, water, which is fluid, and steam, which is vapor. Each can respectively be compared to our past (fixed), present (fluid) and future (vapor, still shapeless). As we move from moment to moment, or rather each moment moves through us, so we define and create our history which then becomes fixed and already written.

Like the waters of the planet that connect the land masses together, so our blood reaches every part, bringing nutrients and oxygen, and carrying away waste products and carbon dioxide, which we breathe out.

The blood also carries a magnetic charge; attached to its iron content are packages of energy that are delivered to every cell in the body. This is why girls or women who lose a lot of blood during their time of menstruation can become anemic and lethargic, but as soon as they start taking iron, the lost energy soon becomes replenished. When your blood becomes charged with energy, it delivers increased sustenance to every part of your body, including your brain.

Tears are salt water, and like blood, salt contains and holds energy, which is why holy water always has some salt added to it.

98

When we cry, we dispatch emotional energy, which is why we always feel better after a good cry, but also more tired.

The salt water of the planet contains energy; the molecule of salt forms a cube, a crystalline shape that makes it possible to store energy, as if it were contained in a box.

It is not by chance that the Essene Brotherhood, who are said to have been Christ's teachers and mentors, lived in Qumran on the shore of the Dead Sea, the saltiest body of water on Earth. In fact, it is so salty that it is the only place on Earth where nothing organic can survive. The waters of the Dead Sea are know to contain curative powers; you can often see people floating in the salty waters hoping to cure their skin conditions, rheumatism, arthritis and the like.

In Roman times Centurions were paid their wages in salt; harvested on the shore of the Dead Sea, it was a precious commodity, much like gold is today.

Life is continuously offering new opportunities and there are those who prefer to avoid the risk and retreat to old familiar patterns, and those who welcome the challenge and call to adventure. The latter are the people who become famous, rich and successful, even if at first they do not succeed, because they never tire of trying.

Failure leads to success because with every failure a person learns what not to do. It is said that Edison tried over one hundred substances to light up his first commercially viable light bulb, and finally found the right substance—a carbon filament. His message to the world: never give up. Thomas Watson has said that the best way to succeed is to double your rate of failure.

Be like the water, always covering new ground and being flexible in your actions, opinions and desires.

This hexagram brings your attention to the power and healing properties of water. You can make your own holy water by adding a pinch of salt and some energy emanating from your fingers to a small glass of water. This water can then be used to sprinkle around the room when energetically cleaning a space.

The Oracle says:
*Water suggests depth and unpredictability which can
be interpreted in two ways: either as a danger or an
opportunity. Often the unknown appears to be threatening
and dangerous, but when tackled with courage and
persistence, it can yield and transform, to eventually
become a familiar circumstance and a positive experience.*

Exercise:
Think of the first time you entered a new school, college or work
place. It might have felt foreboding or even threatening to begin with,
but within weeks it most probably became manageable and familiar.

Decide to do something you have never done before to
experience the feeling of novelty and to witness the process of the
unfamiliar becoming familiar.

30. BEAUTY
Fire above, Fire below

I t is said that beauty is in the eye of the beholder—what is beautiful to one person might not seem beautiful to another. What is considered beautiful at our stage of history might appear to be ugly a century later. What is beauty? C. K. Norwid, the 19th century Polish poet, said it was the shape of love. If you love something, you will find it to be beautiful. We cling to what we believe gives us nourishment, satisfaction, or joy. For a young child that might be his teddy bear or favorite doll; for an adult it can be a relationship or a favorite memory.

Yet no amount of clinging will cause another person to become part of us. We might share time and experiences together, but our friend's or partner's journey is their own—unique and separate from anybody else's.

The fire that brings people together is the passion, or the passing of ions where the energy exchange between two people is food for them. When they feel passionate about each other, they will both strive for more energy exchange. In every relationship there is an energy field between people and this field is uniquely flavored by the energetic contributions to the relationship by each party.

We develop energy fields with each person we know or have a relationship with. Good energy as well as toxic energy can gather in that field. If we feel tired and depleted after an exchange with another person, it means that they have taken from us more energy than they have contributed to that exchange.

Sometimes we cling to that which is not necessarily good for us out of habit due to addiction. It is a curious phenomenon that we can crave what is bad for us. That is because we have programmed our systems by taking in a toxic substance or energy in the first place. Our body does know what is good for it, but sometimes we lose touch with its needs and become deaf to its voice. Our systems follow our leadership and strive to absorb more of the energy we feed them. They do not have the discernment to know what is right and what is wrong, unless we train them to be sensitive to our real needs.

This hexagram indicates that the fire within—the passion that is resident in every person's soul—can be accessed and channelled to contribute to our creativity and healing. The origin of the understanding about the energy of kundalini was the science of unleashing the inner power. Kundalini is said to reside coiled at the base of the spine until it is aroused, and when awakened, it is said to be sent to the head to trigger enlightenment. When active, it can be directed toward a chosen aim.

The Oracle says:
Learn to listen to your body and it will tell you what it needs. Acknowledge the fire within and learn to enhance the spark of passion. Realize that you are like the sun; learn to share your passion and spread your warmth.

Exercise:
What are you passionate about? How can you develop your passion into a conflagration that can illuminate your life?

Make a list of what you love to do. Decide to spend at least a couple of hours each week doing what you are passionate about, so you can develop your spark of passion into a raging, unstoppable fire that will warm your life.

31. WOOING
Mountain below, Lake above

It is natural for a human to become involved emotionally with another person. There is no cure for love and there is no protection against purely human emotions. Feelings do not wane with age, though mostly people learn to not be carried away by their emotions and to be able to control their behavior.

Being "in love" is a symptom of one's humanity. However, there are many kinds of emotions we might feel for different people at different times. In fact, we can feel varied emotions for many people all at the same time. We are connected by silver threads of energy with each other and if they would ever become visible, we would see the Earth covered in a dense web of thin energy gossamer, spanning from person to person, from city to city, from country to country. The threads connect all continents and all landmasses—wherever there are people, there are feelings—both high and low.

We humans are capable of making choices and choosing to discard the low feelings. If Othello had decided to not give in to jealousy, Desdemona would still be alive at the end of the play and love would triumph. We can decide to contribute to love's victory, if we reject greed, avarice, jealousy and all the vices that attempt to hold us in their grip. All energies want to continue to live and are looking for hosts who are willing to offer them a home. But some energies live higher up the levels of the astral light and some are lower.

One way to recognize the difference between a vice and virtue is that a vice comes uninvited, when we are vulnerable, weak and at a low point in our energetic life; virtues come when they are invited or summoned, and when we work to bring them into our life and energy field to share our energetic space. They come when they recognize our behaviors and see that they are akin to their own energetic make-up. For example, truth or courage will live with us if we uphold the truth and behave courageously.

There are people we feel close to, like our family, lovers and best friends, but there are also those who might not like us, or whom we "rub up the wrong way," or who are difficult to get along with. But every person alive today is here for a reason, even if we do not know what that reason is, and even if they themselves do not yet know what that reason is. When you look into another person's eyes, you are connecting to their soul, which is dedicated to preserving their life and helping them identify their life mission. Every person's soul comes from the same tribe of souls, so, in a way, we are all related. However, not everyone you cross paths with wishes to be your friend or wants the best for your life.

The greeting "namaste" says, "My spirit recognizes the spirit in you." It is a declaration of respect for another person and the fact that they are a spiritual being, jut like we all are.

So be discerning in your choice of friends and choose your relationships wisely. Find your soul tribe—those people who treat you with respect, people you can learn from and whom you have reason to respect as well.

One way to find out if the person you are meeting respects you and your time is to see if they keep you waiting at the arranged meeting time or are they on time.

The combination of the lake and the mountain brings together height and depth—two opposites that when combined offer a whole range of experiences. Both are to do with the magical, mystical side of life, exploring spirituality and the inner depths of the human soul. The mountain reaches toward the heavens and becomes veiled in mists and clouds, while the lake reaches inward to the hidden recesses of experience and the source of a person's emotions, often initiated during childhood and still influential during adulthood.

It is time to let old wounds and hurts go and to be open to new adventures and new relationships.

This hexagram says there is someone in your environment who deserves your attention and your time. It could be someone you just met or someone you have known for a long time, but perhaps have neglected to communicate with for a while.

The Oracle says:
You might be surprised who your real friends are. You have more friends than you realize.

Exercise:
Make a list of people who you think belong to your soul tribe—those who make you feel comfortable and bring out the best in you. Make the decision to treat these people with respect and to foster your relationship with them by regularly communicating with them.

32. CONSTANCY
Wind below, Thunder above

To make a success out of any situation or to cause a desire to be fulfilled, one needs to be constant. Natural growth follows the energetic trace of constancy. A plant grows through many small efforts; a child grows in tiny, unnoticeable increments; a tree grows over a number of years.

When we take on a project or set about achieving a goal, we should remember that a thousand small efforts in the same direction is a better course of action than one huge effort, and then nothing until the next attempt. In his book, *The Outliers**, Malcolm Gladwell postulates that in order to achieve mastery and success in anything, one needs to give it a thousand hours in training. He quotes numerous examples where successful people had practiced their art or craft for numerous hours and days before achieving fame and fortune in their chosen field.

Sometimes it seems as if fame and success can come to a person overnight, but this is not so. If you check out their history, they had worked for a long time for the recognition they eventually receive. In his book *On Writing*** Stephen King describes how his fame and fortune came when he sold the movie rights to the story described in his book *Carrie*. In *On Writing* he admits that he writes ever single day, even on Christmas and other holidays. (He also admits that he

---

**The Outliers: The Story of Success*, Malcolm Gladwell, Little, Brown & Company, 2008

***On Writing: A Memoir of the Craft*, Stephen King, Charles Scribner's Sons, 2000 had told reporters that he does take a break on Christmas day, but that was just to satisfy their curiosity and incredulity at his constancy in pursuing his craft.)

Natural growth is constant and what this hexagram is pointing to is the need for an ongoing effort in the direction of your dreams. There is a point in any endeavor when it is easy to give up because the effort seems arduous and appears never to end. They say the darkest hour is just before the dawn. Completing a task is like climbing a hill or a mountain—once you get to the top, the journey down becomes easier. Once you can see the end and get a sense of the finished product, you can relish the feeling of accomplishment, awaiting at the finish line.

In the author's experience as a writer, there is a moment after a book is more than half finished that I get an energy boost because I can now see and feel the finish line.

Constancy is habit forming—through repetition we build our habits until they become part of our make-up and character. Habits and mastership are formed in four stages:

1. When you decide to learn or to do something new, like learning to play the piano, learning a new language, inhaling your first cigarette, or beginning to play a game, like cards, Scrabble or football, you know the piano exists, you have seen a football game on television, you have been around smokers, but you don't really know yet what is involved. This is the known unknown.

2. Then you start your lessons and you get an idea what is involved. You touch the piano keys and you are shown some simple scales. At first you have a little bit of experience—you can put your first sentences together in a foreign language, but you have to think about it and it all seems so difficult as you struggle to remember the vocabulary. Many people who sign up to learn a new skill, like to speak a foreign language, or how to play an instrument, give up at this stage.

3. Then you can begin to speak, you can play melodies, you

can read notes. You understand the rules of the game. When you smoke, you no longer cough, you know what to do and how to do it. But you still have to think about what you are doing; it is not yet "second nature" to you. When speaking a foreign language your sentences are haltingly slow and awkward, because you have to think about every word and phrase. However, you can now express yourself so that you are understood.

4. Finally, the activity you have learned is part of your energetic make-up and you no longer have to think about what you are doing. You can play the piano without looking at your hands; when playing football, your legs seem to know where to take you without a conscious thought. Smoking is now a habit which is difficult to break; you reach for a cigarette without thinking. This is the stage when a person becomes really skilled and the new habit no longer involves our conscious thinking, but is a throughout process, involving all parts. This is the known known.

Constancy allows a person to make the journey from the known unknown to the known known. Accompanied by persistence, constancy supports a person in their learning process.

Constancy is a trait that allows another person to be secure that you will not suddenly change or become dangerous or unpredictable in any way. It is offering another person the stability of knowing that you are reliable. However, it does not mean that you will not change; it is simply a guarantee of standards upheld and of courtesy and respect maintained. If it signified no change, constancy would become stagnation. After all, the one constant in our lives is change!

Constancy is a benchmark, an energy frequency you radiate and become known for. When you meet new people, they look for qualities, attitudes and behaviors they can rely on in their association with you.

Constancy is a quality that allows a person to grow other qualities. If a person wishes to become patient, for example, and they add constancy to their efforts, they will indeed become patient. So constancy can help build good habits. The bad habits are never associated with constancy. You do not say, "He is constant in his gambling." More likely you would say that a person is possessed by their bad habits. So constancy is associated with conscious choice, rather than giving up one's right to choose. It is self-induced and self-determined. If you want to be known as a patient, trustworthy, hard-working, or honest person, simply add constancy to any of the above-mentioned adjectives, and you will become constant in your efforts to invite your chosen qualities into your life so you can become the person you are striving to be.

Constancy is a universal quality because the universe is constant. So whenever constancy fails us, we can follow the example of the Northern Star and become re-inspired to become constant in our endeavors.

Wind and thunder together predict that a storm is coming. The changes might appear to be dramatic, but if you have a long view and embrace the inevitable transformation that is coming your way, you can benefit from the fresh opportunity that will be opening up after the storm. Real warriors of the energetic kind thrive during the storm and come out of the turbulence unscathed. The scenery will change, old friends will move far away, prosperous businesses will hit on hard times, but an indomitable spirit will prevail.

In this hexagram, a person is caught between the wind and the thunder, and both can appear to be threatening and difficult to overcome. But a successful person sees obstacles as challenges and turns temporary setbacks into opportunities. Unlike the quiet before a storm, this is a time when a lot is happening and change is imminent. In amidst the difficulties and the challenges, an opportunity is opening up— it can lead, if applied with good intentions, to other greater new beginnings.

The Oracle says:
Spot the opportunity that presents itself to you under the guise of a problem or a challenge. Once spotted, seize it, so that it may reveal to you your next step.

Exercise:
Write down all the problems, difficulties, challenges you are facing at the moment. Then, next to each one, write down what you need to do to overcome them. From these solutions create a "to do" list, prioritizing your most urgent needs first. Keep this list close by you and cross out each item as it becomes accomplished.

33. RETREAT
Mountain below, Heaven above

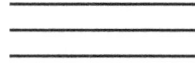

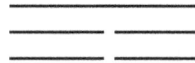

Going toward something, like a destination or a goal, means retreating from something else. As a person makes their choices and decides what they want, they will attempt to exclude from their life everything that is the opposite of their desires and that which stops them from achieving their goals.

Sometimes, however, there needs to be a retreat from the pursuit of one's goals, not to start a new mission, but to pause and take a look at where one is going and whether your life is on track to achieve what you came here to Earth to achieve. There are certain times in life when a retreat is called for, especially during, or soon after, the mid-life, when one's life's path begins to take shape and points toward a direction already established in one's younger years.

The best way to have a retreat is to change the surrounding scenery, like going to another city or another country. When one is in unfamiliar surroundings, one tends to be more alert, and more open to new ideas. There are people who go on silent retreats, or even retreats that are held in complete darkness. This allows a person to journey inward and to discover what one really wants and how one can become one's own guide in order to create the most satisfying and fulfilling life one can.

Darkroom retreats have been used by a variety of spiritual traditions throughout the centuries as a higher-level practice. The aspirant enters a room specially prepared to admit absolutely no light and spends a number of days under this sensory deprivation in order to bring about a profound shift of consciousness.

Research has shown that in prolonged darkness a biochemical

reaction in the brain causes altered states of perception, allowing for accelerated evolution and a better understanding of one's spiritual path.

However, retreat does not need to be so extreme as to require a person to sit in darkness for a week, a fortnight or 40 days; it is sufficient to carve out some time to look at one's life and one's goals, to better define the road ahead.

This hexagon suggests we look at our life from the standpoint of working for our goals and retreating from the obstacles that stand in our way. Are we on the right path? Or do we need to make some adjustments in our life so we can become more clear about what it is that we want to achieve in this life? To look carefully at our life so far and plan ahead for the next stage that is already on its way, it is a good idea to go away from our familiar surroundings for a few days.

The Oracle says:
Always retreat from darkness and choose the light. If you feel someone has a negative influence upon you, find ways to retreat from them, even if it means causing a temporary upset or recrimination.

Exercise:
Plan a brief retreat, say an evening, in which you turn off the phone and do not turn on the television. Think about you life so far and write a few sentences to describe it. Then project forward and write a paragraph or two about where you would want it to go next and how you are hoping your life will unfold.

34. GREAT STRENGTH
Heaven below, Thunder above

here does great strength come from? Who has it? Think of the mother who has the strength to lift a car so she can rescue her child who has been trapped underneath it. Think of the man who stands against the convictions of a whole village or even a town because he believes that what he is doing is right. We all have great strength within us, but it takes belief, conviction and commitment to bring it out. Above all, it will manifest when a person is acting on behalf of others, not just for himself (or herself).

When do you feel at your strongest? It has to be when you believe in yourself and what you can do. To build great strength this is a good place to start—to grow and enhance one's belief in oneself. There are several ways to do this because there are several sources of strength from which we can replenish our own. Here are a few ideas:

1. Add up what are the chances for you to be born at the time you were born to the parents you were born to? What were the chances for your mother to meet your father? What were the chances for them to get together? What were the chances for them to conceive you? What were the chances for your mother to carry you to full term? What were the chances for you to be fed, clothed, educated, nurtured and loved so that you could successfully grow up to be the person you are today, able to read this book?

2. Great strength can come from what you can do. It took time to learn to walk, read, write, drive a car, dance, cook, draw. Make a list

113

of what you can do and own it. Be proud of your achievements so far and any successes that are still to come.

3. Great strength can come from what you know. Throughout your life you have learned about history, geography, politics, human behavior, gardening, using computers and other equipment. Think of all the places you have been, all the challenges you have successfully met and mastered, and all the people you know.

4. Great strength can come from who you are—your character formation and the many qualities you have acquired throughout your life. What are they? Are you generous, patient, punctual, optimistic, loving, or giving? When you enter a room you bring those qualities with you. The more conscious you are about who you are and the many virtues you represent, the more you become self-confident and radiate that belief within every encounter with every person you meet.

This hexagram suggests that there is great strength within you. Find ways to own it so you can become a better person who is on an evolutionary path throughout your life, getting better every day.

The Oracle says:
There are many kinds of strength. Being true to oneself is a good place to start when building one's strength. Once you connect to your mission and sense of purpose, you will discover many other strengths that will illuminate your path ahead and tell you what you need to do, or be, next.

Exercise:
Make a list of your strengths. Then decide to turn one of your perceived weaknesses into a strength.

35. PROGRESS
Earth below, Fire above

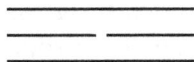

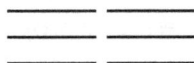

What is progress and how do you measure it? When you get up in the morning, do you check whether you have progressed as you move from the previous day or week into the present? As you pass through your now between the past and your future, how do you describe your current position in your life's journey?

According to this hexagram, the fire is already lit and it is supported by the earth. Your life and your chosen path are being nurtured by the five foods, by the loving people around you, like your family and friends, and by the passage of time.

One way to look at progress is to imagine that the path to your goal is like a train journey, and that along the way there are seven stations. This image allows you to break up the journey into segments, so the distance does not seem so daunting. You can then give each station a name so that when you arrive at each of the seven destinations, you confirm to yourself that you are really on your way.

Say your goal is to earn a certain amount of money. You can give each station a numerical name, so that when you get a rise or take on additional work, you can confirm to yourself that you are indeed progressing.

Say your goal is to write a book. You can give your stations the names of your chapters. You can have more (or fewer) than seven stations; seven was just an example. You can also make a drawing of your train journey and as you achieve each part, you can draw the train arriving at the next station. It is always a good idea to confirm one's achievements so that the journey does not seem so insurmountable. A visual aid, like a train journey or a vision board help cement the idea of what it is you want to achieve in your life.

Sometimes we feel we have come across a road block and that not much progress is happening. That is the time to make progress happen. The progress you make to overcome a block does not even have to be related to the project you are currently working on. It is just important at these times to introduce into your life some kind of progress; any progress. You can clean out a drawer or do the laundry; it does not matter. Just give yourself a small (or large) success so you can move on with your chosen tasking.

The suffix -gress comes from Latin, where it has the meaning *step* or *move*. This meaning is found in such words as: aggression, congress, digress, egress, ingress, progress, regress, transgress. Each of these words indicates movement—each day you can either move toward or away from your goal.

As any older person will tell you, time is short, and now is the time when you can make a difference, both in your own life and in the life of other people.

This hexagram supports your progress in the direction of your chosen goal. Progress is always possible. You need to have a dream so that you can have a dream come true, as the song teaches us.

The Oracle says:
You are the wisest you have ever been; you are the youngest you will ever be. So act now, for your time is now.

Exercise:
Create a vision board. Be bold and have all your wildest dreams represented in picture form. Keep it visible so you can look at it often.

116

36. DARKENING OF THE LIGHT, PERSECUTION
Fire below, Earth above

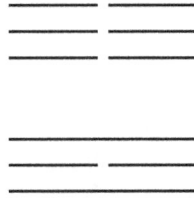

This is a time when everything seems a little vague. What was clear in the beginning is no longer obvious, as if a large shadow had obscured the light. Every life goes through stages like this when the questions seem to keep coming up: "What am I doing?" "Why am I doing it?" "What is it all for?" Perhaps this is not the best time to attempt to answer these questions because the response can only come back to, "I don't know." However, keep on going because the light will return. Just as there is a natural division on planet Earth between day and night, and there are times that are the in-between times, called dawn and dusk, there are moments, or in fact whole years, when everything seems to stand still. Of course this is an illusion because nothing ever stands still—movement is always occurring underground, unseen and unnoticed. These are good times to look after one's health and one's maintenance, because when the light returns and everything becomes clearer again, there might not be enough time to look after the basics in such a thorough way. In these balsamic* times it is possible to gather oneself in preparation for busier times ahead.

It is also important to remember that the fire is still there, but it has gone underground. One can attempt to bring it back to the surface by remembering one's initial inspiration, one's aims and goals. According to the dictionary persecution is hostility and

---

*In astrology the balsamic phase of the moon is receptive and releasing. It is about letting go of the past and turning one's thoughts and attention to the future.

ill-treatment, especially because of race or political or religious beliefs. It can apply to one's feelings of being wronged by another person, for whatever reason. Sometimes it can just be our imagination, but sometimes persecution can be a very real obstacle in one's life.

In order to progress, this is a situation that has to be dealt with. Sometimes persecution or ill-treatment is a result of a lack of communication. It can often be resolved by having a conversation with the other person and by genuinely and truthfully sharing one's feelings with another. If this is not possible, and the other person does not want to talk, it might be best to walk away from the situation and exclude the other person from one's circle of friends.

The light darkens when night falls, but the sun will rise again in the morning. Every life has its dark moments and bright patches; it is important to always value and look for the light. Creation does not persecute us, only other people can do that. Creation is loving and supportive and we are its children. It is much more powerful than any person who might not wish us well.

This hexagram reminds us of the good times and the many supportive energies that are all around us.

The Oracle says:
Store up for yourself the good times so that you can refer to them often and be reminded of the energetic sustenance that is possible when you connect to the fire that is within you.

Exercise:
Write down five of your happiest experiences so far and hold them in your memory like precious gems that preserve the light. Take these gems out and polish them often so they can help you weather the darker times.

37. FAMILY
Fire below, Wind above

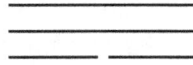

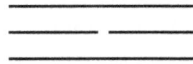

Our family is much more than just our blood relations. In fact, we have several tribes that we belong to—there is also our soul tribe and our spiritual companions, some of whom we might not yet be aware of. There are almost eight billion people on Earth and we will never meet them all. But become aware of those who do cross your path. People are often drawn together like magnets and there might be a reason why you work with the people you work with or why you meet specific people at specific times. Similar energies can be aphrodisiac to each other and inevitably pull towards each other until they connect and meet.

Learn to read the signs and other people's compatibility with your own energy field. You never know who will have the next piece of advice for you that can change your life, or who will be able to connect you with exactly the right person at the right time when you are in need of a new job, a joint venture, or a friend. People do like to help others (don't you?) and will be there for you, but you need to learn how to ask. This is a difficult thing to do, because mostly we are brought up to be strong, self-sufficient and self-reliant. But when you learn to ask, you will be surprised who comes to the rescue. Often it is not your family or close circle of friends. Mark Granovetter*, American sociologist at Stanford University, coined the phrase "the strength of weak ties." What it refers to is that those we are close with have the same connections we do and are often not willing or

Granovetter, M. (1983). *The Strength of Weak Ties: A Network Theory Revisited*. Sociological Theory 1: 201–233 capable of helping us find what we need outside of their and our sphere of influence. However, it is often the stranger, the chance encounter, or the new acquaintance (in other words, the "weak tie") that will have the solution or the connection that we need.

Family and clan are two different entities. The former suggests blood connections, whereas the latter indicates a soul connection. We connect to other people through religious congregations, educational facilities and places of work. Each place where we meet people can become a place where we meet someone who is going to become a significant part of our life. The whole world is full of potential friends, business partners, romantic interests and people who might just have an idea or piece of advice that will set our life on a new path.

There is a theory that we are connected to everyone on Earth through a maximum of six personal connections. This idea is known as *six degrees of separation*. It is also known as the *Six Handshakes* rule. As a result, a chain of "a friend of a friend" can be traced to connect any two people in a maximum of six steps.

This hexagram suggests you keep an open mind when meeting new people. Do not hesitate to discuss with others your ideas and plans; they might just have an idea that will help you move onto the next step in your journey.

The Oracle says:
You are not alone. There are many people whom you know and not yet know that wish to help you.

Exercise:
Think of all the people you know. Multiply that (approximate) number by the number of people they know, and again, multiplying that number six times. Say you know 1,000 people, and each of them knows 1,000 more; that is already a million. Step two brings that number up to a thousand million. You can easily include everyone on Earth if you carry on the multiplication for another four calculations.

38. OPPOSITION, DIVERGENCE
Fire above, Lake below

Once a connection to another person or a situation is established and maintained, separation from it can be painful. On the other hand, it can be a relief to become separated from an abusive or difficult situation. Life is full of beginnings and separations. When we become a teenager, we are separated from the ways and energies of childhood. When we are adult, we usually become separated from our parents and from the parental home.

Divergence could refer to the path less travelled, when we deliberately separate ourselves out from the crowd. One of the best pieces of advice a young person can receive is to go their own way when the mob is on the move in another direction. Do not be a part of the crowd; find your own unique path. After all, you are unique and there is no one else on Earth with the exact same fingerprints as you.

If we become too attached to another person or a situation, separation can be difficult. Even the death of a pet can cause grief and misery. If we take on the role to be stewards to a cat or dog, we must realize that these pets do not live as long as we do, and at some point in the future we will have to bid the animal goodbye.

Losing a spouse can cause years of grief and sadness. It can help if the person left behind believes in life after death and that their husband or wife is still alive on another plane. Many people have written and spoken about instances in which they were in communication with their loved ones "on the other side." In many countries altars dedicated to family ancestors are erected in the home and fresh fruit and other morsels are put out regularly to feed the deceased members of the family.

Losing a parent is the natural course of events, and yet this, too, can be the cause of grief. When someone close to us dies, we think about our encounters with them and often regret that perhaps we had not been as nice to them as we could have been and perhaps have not said we loved them as often as we could have. Grief is a natural process and it is simply giving back to the deceased the energy that they had given us during their lifetime. They will need it on the next stage of their journey, so it is important to let it go back to the source of its arising, and not to hold onto it.

This hexagram confirms that in the course of a lifetime there are many separations; it is inevitable that we will grieve the loss of a parent or a friend (or both). It s important to consider that we might be reunited with our ancestors, parents and siblings when our own life on Earth is over.

The Oracle says:
Follow your unique path and know that you are not alone and simply never will be. You are loved and protected, and there are those in the spirit world who will always look after you.

Exercise:
Write a letter to a deceased friend or parent. Let them know how you felt about them when they were alive and thank them for their friendship or their nurturing ways.

39. ADVERSITY
Mountain below, Water above

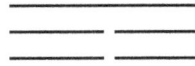

Obstructions are on every path; no one's journey through life is smooth and without pitfalls. Obstructions are there to be overcome and surmounted. They are challenges to take in our stride, and they are lessons that teach us about ourselves and how we handle challenges.

We must not be stopped. Our journey must progress and take its natural course. It is a measure of our intelligence and ingenuity how we overcome obstructions. They are like a test, and although sometimes we feel that we are facing them alone, the truth is that we are not. There is always someone or some energy watching and waiting to see what we do and how we manage it. Once we overcome an obstruction, we reap the rewards of the continuing journey and the experience of having done it. It might not feel like much of an achievement, but it is. Healing after an illness, recovery after an injury, or coming back to a sense of equilibrium in oneself are all important achievements that we accomplish with the help of our greatest ally—ourselves. Small victories on the way provide us with self-esteem and belief in ourselves.

Our bodies know how to heal; our soul knows how to bring us back to a sense of purpose and wellbeing. All we have to do to support and expedite this process is to be patient, to provide the systems with nourishment, and to be willing to give ourselves time, rather than forever demanding new and greater results.

If we could see our so-called enemies as our friends, we would be able to overcome any difficult situation created by another person with ease. Work with other people, rather than against them.

If you do not understand why another person does what they do, ask them to explain their reasoning. You might be surprised by what they have to say to you. Not every person thinks the way you do, so you can learn from another person's point of view.

Develop a long view about your life and your mission. If you keep your eyes looking long distance, the obstructions on the way will appear smaller and easy to navigate though.

This hexagram invites you to see your problems as a learning and a challenge to be overcome. If you have difficulty getting over an adversity, ask for help. You might be surprised how many people are willing to help you in your hour of need. You have mighty friends both on Earth and within the realms of energy.

The Oracle says:
Be gentle with yourself and treat yourself kindly, as you would a child. Sometimes you just need to trust that everything you need to achieve success is already within you, ready and willing to serve.

Exercise:
If an angel or a genie appeared before you at this moment, what would be your three wishes? Write them down and re-look at what you have written in a month's time. See if any of your wishes have been fulfilled. If not, check again in another month's time. Keep checking every month until your desires come to pass.

40. DELIVERANCE, RELEASE
Water below, Thunder above

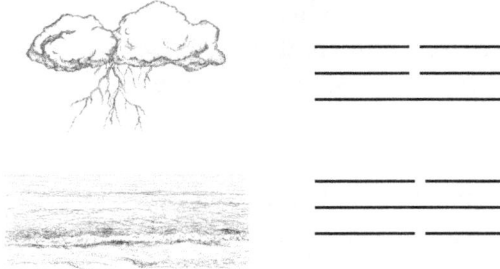

Deliverance is always at hand. Ask, and you shall be given. You are not alone. All around you are forces and energies that support your life and want to help you on your journey.

Deliverance suggests delivery. Something—some higher energy or intelligence—delivers us from harm or from evil, as in the *Lord's Prayer*. It is a word that is not used so much these days; if this prayer were to be written today we might say something like "protect," or "shelter me from evil."

However, the word *deliver*, unlike *shelter* or *protect*, has an active quality to it. It suggests a mighty hand reaching out, picking a person up and taking them away from a challenging situation into safety and out of harm's way.

Release, on the other hand, has a different connotation. It speaks of being free after a period of imprisonment or after having lost one's freedom. It has within it a sense of liberation and the dropping away of one's bonds or shackles.

There are many times in life when we might feel a lack of freedom, although sometimes the limits imposed upon us can be of our own choosing. For example, when we decide to have children and then spend many years looking after them, feeding them, planning their education, and finally helping them become established in the world, we might feel that we haven't got the time or energy to pursue our own interests. Or perhaps we have a job which helps us pay our way but is so demanding that we feel that our freedom has been impaired.

Then there are those special times in life when the shackles drop away and once more we are free to choose our own unique path. Perhaps the child (or children) have left home, or the job has come to an end. Whatever the reason, it is the energy of release that makes itself known at these times and gives us the freedom to fully feel ourselves and to make new choices which previously had not been possible. Cherish these times and make the most of them.

This hexagram indicates that this could be a time when opportunity beckons. The universe issues a permission and it is now possible to make a quantum leap forward.

The Oracle says:
Be fearless in your dreams so you can be fearless in your life.

Exercise:
If you could have anything you wanted and be anything you wanted to be, what would it be? Imagine you already have what you have wanted and are what you wanted to be. Feel it, smell it, hear it, be it.

41. DECREASE
Lake below, Mountain above

Sometimes we live within the cycle of increase and sometimes we enter the cycle of decrease. One cannot say that one is good and the other bad; it all depends which cycle supports your goal. Sometimes we need to get rid of what we have in order to move on; at other times we need to acquire more to expand.

Acquisition can refer to material possessions, like a home, a car, or other objects that support our education or our life's journey; other times acquisition can refer to knowledge or information. It can also refer to a relationship—throughout our life we acquire friends, colleagues, acquaintances, lovers, partners. At other times we lose people we are close to, either because we move away from each other, we have a falling out, or people die, or we simply lose touch for lack of effort. It is almost as if there was a revolving door through which different people enter our life or exit at different times. Sometimes there are many people within our sphere of influence; sometimes there are few.

Whatever the substance of our acquisitions, it is important to realize that it is always changing and to be grateful for those who are currently sharing our life.

Life consists of a series of cycles. Times of decrease connect to new cycles which offer growth and increase, just as times of increase connect to cycles of decrease. Sometimes it is possible to make a choice: do you want more to add to your schedule or would you prefer to slow down and have some time for rest and repair?

During the time of decrease, one can sometimes feel that not enough is happening, that time is moving too slowly, and that people around you are not being active enough. These are the "balsamic" times and because they never last, it is wise to take advantage of them and to enjoy the pauses between activities. It is a time to recuperate and to heal, and to gather one's energy to launch into the next period of increase, which is following not far behind the cycle of decrease.

One way to make our time productive and to keep the energy flowing again when we feel stuck in a rut is to deliberately cause a decrease in our life. This is done by going through our possessions and getting rid of what we no longer need. There may be things lurking in our drawers that we have forgotten are still there, like old letters, notes or cards. There may be books on our shelves that we will never read again, or clothes we will never wear again.

The combination of the lake and the mountain brings together height and depth. The mountain rises toward heaven, with its peak in the clouds, nearer to the sun than any other place on Earth. The lake is dark and mysterious and hides many secrets, some of which might become visible in the time of decrease.

This hexagram warns about times of decrease and explains that our lives are like breathing: there are times of decrease and times of increase. It is important to view the times of decrease as a trimming in preparation for what is next.

The Oracle says:
We tend to surround ourselves with too much stuff. Look at everything around you in your home and see if you really need it. If not, there are five ways of dealing with your things: give them away, sell them, throw them away, recycle them, or keep them.

Exercise:
One way to deal with old clothes is to look in your closet and pick out clothes you have not worn for at least a year. Put them in a bag and add a sticker with the date on it and leave them there for six months or a year. If you have not missed them throughout six months or a year, now is a good time to get rid of them.

42. INCREASE
Thunder below, Wind above

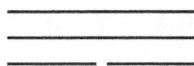

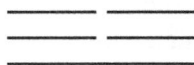

When we are in the cycle of increase, it is important to remember that increase will not last forever and that decrease will follow. By the same token, when in the cycle of decrease, it is important to remember that it will not last forever and that increase will follow.

Increase is a state of affairs, and because it is a time when one is added to (either materially, or energetically, or both), one can easily become overwhelmed. There is much to do—it is a time of trying to keep up with the demands that inevitably come during the time of increase.

It can be difficult to manage all the things that one needs to look after during the period of increase. One thought that can bring some relief is the fact that a period of increase never lasts long and a period of decrease will inevitably follow. When it does, it will be a time to regroup, regather one's strengths and have time to take stock of one's situation. Here one can take comfort from the proverb often quoted by the Sufi poets, "This too will pass."

Increase is a demanding time—it can feel like one's energies are being used up while one is trying to just keep going. This is the time to make sure one has the proper nutrition—both energetically and within the foods one eats, and the supplements one consumes, to replenish the energies that one tends to use up fast within this demanding cycle.

This is a time of extra activity—new people are entering your life, or perhaps new work is coming your way. Demands are being made and new adventures beckon. Within this busy time remember to carve out for yourself some time to meditate, to think, and to plan ahead. Having a long view of one's goals is helpful in weathering these busy times. Although we might sometimes feel overwhelmed and that the demands placed upon us are just too much, we are never required to take on what we cannot handle.

Wind and thunder together predict turbulence. But together with the possible upheaval they both bring, there is also a breath of fresh air blowing through the district and shifting stagnant energies. This is a time to sweep clean and re-evaluate what you are doing and who you are giving your time and energy to.

This hexagram tells us that we are more capable than we had suspected and asks us to embrace this newfound capability with alacrity and enjoyment.

The Oracle says:
You are in service to Creation, and Creation wants you to be the best you can be. The best way to progress to the next level is to fill out the level you are currently on.

Exercise:
Make a list of all the people in your life you are grateful for. Then think of a lesson or a quality each of the people on your list has brought into your life, and why. Write it down next to their name. Then add a reason why this lesson or quality has been important to you on your life's journey.

43. BREAKTHROUGH
Heaven below, Lake above

ithin every life there are moments of breakthrough. This is when, rather than continuing on the wheel which leads from decrease to increase and back to decrease, one is able to switch wheels and energetically move into a higher elevation. This new cycle will have within it its own increase and decrease, but these will occur within a very different cycle and within different timings. Like wheels connected to wheels, there are moments when one can seize the opportunity to elevate into higher realms, but timing is crucial. These opportunities to shift gear appear and then disappear, sometimes never to reappear again, and sometimes to reappear only after a whole new cycle is gone through.

It is important to take advantage of these opportunities when they arise, providing one can recognize they are occurring when they summon one to action. Sometimes a new opportunity can make itself known within a dream; sometimes it can be a recommendation from a friend, or one can hear about it from a chance encounter.

Pay attention to suggestions from other people, not necessarily to blindly follow what other people suggest we do, but to become aware of those opening doors as they become ajar and await our decision to push them further open and to walk through.

Sometimes we will make mistakes and push at the doors that are not yet open, but it is better to learn from such mistakes than to miss the opportunities that are waiting for our reaction. Within every life there are doors that open and doors that close. Do not regret it when it seems that you have missed an opportunity that had promised to lead to an improvement in your life. For every missed opportunity there are scores of new possibilities opening up every day. Be on the lookout for these new openings and have an eye on the next level within whatever it is that you do. Life is potentially an evolutionary journey, so as we age we have the opportunity to become wiser and more skilled at what we do.

The final breakthrough comes at the end of life when we will have achieved everything we have been able to achieve and proceed to our next life.

This hexagram encourages a person to seize the many opportunities their life offers them. Listen to your inner guide and ask for help so you can recognize the important decisions you will need to make to improve and to find those paths that lead to success.

The Oracle says:
Take courage and realize that there is help available. There are people keen to give you good advice and there are unseen friends who will speak through other people or give you a sign that you can recognize. When you are confronted with an important decision, ask yourself whether it opens up new possibilities.

Exercise:
When confronted with an important decision, write down the pros and contras for each choice. Then ignore what you have written and try to imagine that each side of the equation has come to pass. How does it feel? As you look for your new breakthrough, try to combine both thinking and feeling in your decision making process.

44. ENCOUNTER
Wind below, Heaven above

How many people have you known in your life? Think of all the people at school, friends you made on holidays, colleagues at your various workplaces, dates, partners, lovers, teachers, family members, and all those people you have met only briefly, spoken to them for a moment, or bought something from them. There must be thousands. These thousands know and have met thousands more, and so on, until the whole world is covered with people whose life we have touched, either directly or indirectly. Every new person we meet adds to our energy experience. The more people we meet and greet, the more we become acquainted with the great variety and energy content that the human race represents.

We will meet someone today, tomorrow or in the near future, and this person will have a positive impact upon our life, if we let them. So listen carefully to what they have to say; it could change your life for the better. It might not be a big change, but even a small change can bring about dramatic consequences in the long run.

Think of an event or an encounter that has changed your life. Perhaps it was your first meeting with your future spouse, or finding an ad in the newspaper or on line that led to a new job. Perhaps someone had made a suggestion that led to a new career or successful joint venture partnership. These events could feel insignificant at the time but bring about dramatic changes in your life.

Future opportunities might appear just as insignificant but then offer a wealth of new experiences. So be vigilant and look out for those small events and encounters that lead to important shifts in your life.

While we are alive on planet Earth we are part of the human race. What we do here, how we think, and the energies we connect to can either enhance or hinder humanity in its evolutionary process. Often we do not think that our actions or our thoughts matter, but they do contribute to the human story.

This hexagram reminds us that we are members of the human family and asks us to consider our life's legacy while we still have time to achieve what we were meant to achieve in this life.

The Oracle says:
You are part of a greater whole. What you do, think and feel is written into the energetic history of this planet. Be mindful of your next action, thought and intention.

Exercise:
Write down a list of people you have met in your life: your parents, friends, co-workers, colleagues, acquaintances. How many are there? How many people have you influenced and how many have influenced you?

45. GATHERING
Earth below, Lake above

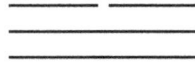

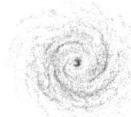

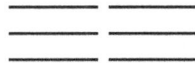

T̶hroughout our life we gather energies into our energy field. We then disperse them as we process them, adding to them our own unique flavor on the way. As energies come through us and radiate from us out into the world, a small amount lingers behind and becomes part of our energetic make-up or character formation. Just like water flowing through a pipe—a few droplets will remain to flavor the next flow of water, or whatever other liquid might be passing through the pipe next.

Every day is a new opportunity to add to the flow of energy passing through us. If we just follow our regular routine, think our regular thoughts, and proceed with our regular actions, there will be nothing new accumulating in our energetic make-up. However, we were made for innovation, discovery and new learning. Our memory capacity is vast and there are people on the planet who speak many languages or acquire a number of skills. We can be as versatile as they are, and as we increase our store of knowledge and reference, our ability to know more and do more increases as well.

We were created to be part of an evolutionary process, so if we want to contribute to this universal trend, we need to push our boundaries and discover what else we can know and do, apart from what we already know and have already achieved. The human will not grow a new arm or evolve wings so that we can fly, but our brain has a large capacity with room to grow. We use only a small percentage of this marvelous organ, and it is for each one of us to increase its capability and develop our five senses so that they can feed us new understandings and new revelations with which to pioneer our next adventure and discover our new abilities.

Each of our five senses has its energetic counterpart. We can learn to see, hear, touch, smell and taste the energies around us. It is only a question of developing the sensitivity to be able to register a range of sensations that go beyond our physical sensitivities.

This hexagram is an encouragement to develop new sensitivities to the energy worlds. It is a reminder that evolution is not yet complete and that our brain and our senses are capable of much finer results than they are currently producing for our benefit.

The Oracle says:
The human is so much more than we currently know. Clairvoyance, remote viewing, telepathy and healing are all possible.

Exercise:
Close your eyes and with outstretched hands walk around your room. Do you feel the changes in temperature in different parts of the room? Do you perhaps feel tingling in your hands? Make a pair of dowsing rods (see the instruction on YouTube) and try working with them both indoors and out in nature. Notice how the rods react to different energies.

46. ASCENDING
Wind below, Earth above

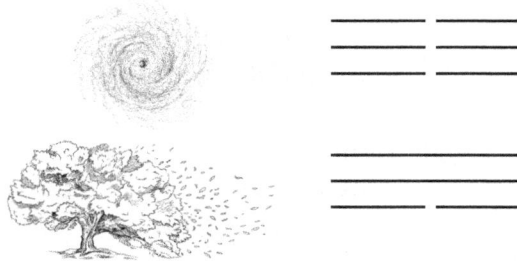

Some people think that aging is a deterioration, and that one's best years are when they are young. But this is not so, because as we age we gather to ourselves experience and wisdom. Life is like climbing a mountain; at first it is difficult and you cannot see where you are going, but once you reach the top, the vista opens up and you can easily see where you are heading to next. Once on top of the mountain—a position that can be likened to one's middle age—there is only one possibility—to descend.

Every age has its own requirements and its own lessons to be learned. The energy associated with each age is different, and as we get older we learn to manage the changes that we keep experiencing throughout life. As we advance up the mountain of life the view keeps changing; as we get closer to the exit, we can look back and see the legacy we are leaving behind. We might be able to find words to describe the journey we have been on and appreciate how different the beginning was as compared to the end.

On the way through life we experience seven distinct energies, and ascend through each waveband, which can be likened to a rainbow or chakra journey. First we experience the fiery red nature of childhood with its unprecedented growth and outgoing energy. Next is orange and the angst and delights of the teenage years. In our twenties we search for independence and new relationships. It is a time of nest building and becoming a parent. Then in green we come to the mid-life, which is like ascending to the top of the mountain. We can see where we have come from and where we are going next, and we feel it is our last chance to make some drastic changes.

Blue, or the menopause (or andropause for men) is a time to distill wisdom from our many experiences, to begin to take account of the future, and to consider who and what we will be leaving behind. The final stages in indigo and violet are a time to make decisions about spirituality, religion and the life that awaits us on the other side of the mountain.

A ship sailing to its destination is rarely on track—small course corrections are needed all the time. We are like this ship, and a wise person keeps an eye on the prize, to see which way he is going and whether he is getting closer to his goals, or further away.

This hexagram instructs you to learn to monitor your energies as you grow older so you can become self-diagnostic regarding your needs and your body's needs.

The Oracle says:
Ever day is an opportunity for advancement. Define the course you are on and decide to steer you ship toward your chosen destination.

Exercise:
Write down three goals: short term, mid-term and long term. Place them where you will look at them often so you can make course corrections on the way.

47. OPPRESSION
Lake above, Water below

As humans we like to be free. We fight for our freedom and oppose laws that restrict it. We see freedom as a precious commodity, and one of the greatest punishments is to take away our freedom and put us in jail.

However, sometimes we limit our own freedom by how we think and act. We can become limited by how we think about ourselves and about what we are capable of. A young child does not yet know what its talents and abilities are, and as we grow older we learn how others respond to us and what we are able to achieve in life. This growing picture of ourselves, as we fill it out throughout the years, remains incomplete because there are always areas within which we could have excelled but did not because of our self-view. There are also areas waiting to be filled in the future, as we grow older and closer to the end of life

The human (every one of us) is capable of so much more than we have already achieved. Past accomplishments are only precursors to our future possibilities. They are a hint of the areas within which we are able to achieve much more. The restrictions we place on ourselves are of our own making; we can become oppressed by our own self-view.

To understand our own qualities and abilities, we can look back on our life and see who and what we have attracted to ourselves over the years. Who are our friends? Who has helped us on our journey? What qualities do they represent? What qualities do they see in us? Why are they attracted to us?

Our relationships speak volumes about ourselves. People

are attracted to others who are similar in their beliefs, actions and thought processes. If people around us represent a high calibre, then perhaps we, too, have similar qualities. If we were our own friend, what would we value about ourselves? These are questions that might help us gain an external view of ourselves, and help us appreciate what we have already achieved.

The next step in this process is to look ahead and begin to see what else we can achieve while being alive here on planet Earth. The journey continues and we can still gather to ourselves qualities and ways of going on that will improve our character and make us a better person.

This hexagram warns against limiting oneself and having a self-view that is based on past mistakes.

The Oracle says:
Do not restrict the view you have of yourself. Keep an open mind and always sstrive to be the best you can be.

Exercise:
Ask ten people who know you to write down your main attributes. Pay special attention to those that are repeated in their responses.

48. THE WELL
Wind below, Water above

Whatever we desire already exists in the world, otherwise we would not be able to desire it. Of course, one could argue that a person might desire to be able to fly like a bird or breathe under water, both of which are not possible without the aid of a flying machine or a submarine. But our real wishes and desires, based in reality and not inspired by fantasy, are achievable and attainable, though perhaps not now, not yet. This realization and the thought that our desires have in fact been already achieved by someone else, elsewhere and at another time, can bring comfort and assurance that yes, we can achieve what we desire.

The well of what is on offer on planet Earth is full—there is enough for everyone. As long as we do not completely destroy our environment, the planet is capable of healing herself and offering renewed resources. We, too, have the incredible ability to pick ourselves up and start again, to not lose hope, and to look to the future for answers to our current predicament, whatever it might be.

Our qualities, skills, experiences and memories are far more precious than objects that make up our material wealth. No one can take these away from us and they become our tools and resources when looking to increase our wealth and wellbeing. So it is important to think about energy first when assessing our standing in the world.

The world might have limited oil reserves, and there might be only a limited amount of gold in the world's gold mines, but there is no limit to how much courage, or confidence, or generosity there is in the energy worlds of the planet. Our energetic well can always be replenished from the experiences of others or from the stories of ancient heroes who overcame impossible odds to bring enlightenment and new revelations into the world.

In studying history, or reading about ancient heroic deeds, try to see what are the energy qualities that people would champion in order to become effective in promoting world change. In thinking about qualities that you admire in others, ask yourself if you might also have those qualities and whether you would want to increase the effectiveness of your actions by adding to those qualities that you already have.

This hexagram indicates that we are all connected to the well of plenty and that whatever qualities we might wish we had, there are great supplies of them available within the energetic well of the planet on which we live.

The Oracle says:
Strive to increase the number of qualities that make up your character.

Exercise:
Write down ten qualities that you know you have. Try to find an example of an action to connect to each of these qualities. Then find ten qualities that you wish you had but don't think you have yet. Try to find ten actions that would embody those qualities and plan to find a way to perform these actions so as to bring these new qualities into your life.

49. REVOLUTION
Fire below, Lake above

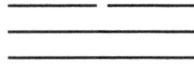

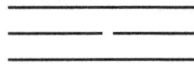

We live in changing times and this hexagram speaks of changes inside leading to changes outside. There comes a time in every person's life when a review is called upon to assess one's life journey so far and to look to future prospects. This happens several times, for example during the years of the mid-life opportunity (between 35 and 45 approximately) or during the menopause years (45 to 55), and then again, in later years. In fact, life is a series of revolutions, adjustments, changes, reviews, questing, questioning and reassessments. But not always do these internal examinations cause an external adjustment of circumstances.

This hexagram is pointing to a situation within which everything is being altered—the mindset, the commitments and ultimately the external circumstances of one's life—relationships, home, career, or spiritual values. It is all evolving, shedding the old and embracing the new. Look back at your childhood and think about the many changes you have undergone in the years since that moment in time. There are physical changes, like growth, hormonal changes, and brain development. There is an accumulation of experiences, and there are many more relationships that have been established throughout the years. In fact, one could say that we are no longer the same person as the child in that early memory. Something else has grown upon us, making us the person we are today.

As the planet goes around the sun every year and comes back to where it was on the day our birth, we celebrate another milestone in our life, known as our birthday. Each year we live through 365 or 366 days and nights, adding to our growing arsenal of experiences.

An adult who is 20 years old will have lived through over 7,300 dawns and dusks, which amounts to more than 175,200 hours. That is a lot of time to begin to achieve one's dreams and to make a mark within the energetic content of the world.

At 40 these numbers double, and at 60 there will have been over 21,900 days within which a person will have gone through a myriad of experiences, changes and evolutions.

This hexagram confirms that transformation is happening all the time, even while you sleep. Decide now what kind of changes you would like to see in your life, so you can begin to take control of your future, rather than having it happen upon you.

The Oracle says:
You are a moving diagram. Rather than fighting the aging process, embrace the changes that are happening in your life and redirect them to reflect the wisdom and experience you are accumulating in an on-going process.

Exercise:
Find a word or phrase to express each stage of the journey you have been through and will be going through in the future: childhood, adolescence, independence, mid-life, seniority and old age.

50. THE NEW
Wind below, Fire above

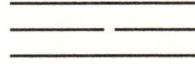

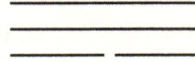

As the winds of change blow through our life, there are many times when we need to adjust to new circumstances. When the two elements of wind and fire come together, the wind fans the fire and the rate of change accelerates. These are times when we might feel overwhelmed by the amount of change happening in our lives.

It could be new relationships, or the end of relationships, illness, death, or the birth of a child. It could be a new career or a new business opportunity. All these changes bring with them their own unique demands and difficulties in adjusting to new circumstances. It is at times like these that we need to give the new circumstance the time for us to settle into a new routine.

The biggest mistake we can make when facing new circumstances and new opportunities is to hold onto the past. The past might represent a comfortability that is known and have recorded within it many good results. However, the moment we become comfortable and are no longer challenged is precisely the time to move on and discover new ways of looking at our life and finding ways to advance in our life's journey.

When taking on a new job, for example, give yourself six months to get to know your co-workers and to become familiar with office routines and timings. There might be computer protocols to learn and your boss's requirements to be fulfilled. There might be lunch places to discover down the street and new friends with whom to share a mid-day meal. All this can seem daunting at first, but soon will become a familiar routine.

Life is a series of new discoveries and continuous adjusting to the new normal. How many times have you looked back at your life and became astonished at the many changes that have occurred throughout the years? If you look forward, by the same token, what are the changes that can still happen? Can you predict what they might be like?

The cauldron of life is continuously being mixed up into new configurations. Some we can predict, like the growing pains and the milestones one goes through in the aging process, like puberty and establishing one's independence in the grown-up world. Others are less predictable and will come upon us unexpectedly. We cannot predict these changes, but we can always be prepared for change in general.

This hexagram assures us that we were made for change. It is a comfort to be ready for change at all times, because then we can avoid the shock that sudden change brings.

The Oracle says:
Get used to change. The biggest change of all will come at the end of your life. If you contemplate your exit from this Earth often, it will not be a shock when that final moment comes.

Exercise:
Look back at your life five years ago. What has changed? What have you accomplished? Write down the main new features that have been established as part of your current life.

51. SHOCK
Thunder below, Thunder above

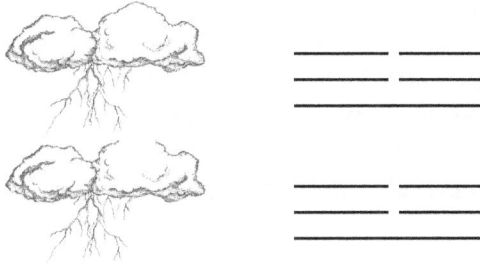

Have you ever jumped when thunder unexpectedly struck close to where you were? Have you ever been shocked when hearing an unexpected noise? Have you ever experienced an earthquake? Remember how it sends a shock through the system and can even cause you to jump, or for your body to start shaking uncontrollably. This is your body preparing you for a flight or fight response, which will persist until you realize the sound is not threatening and you can settle down to whatever you were doing prior to the interruption.

Sometimes our world becomes shaken, though not completely shattered, and our lives seem very fragile at that moment. Throughout our life we receive shocks. Sometimes these can be life changing events, like the death of a loved one or losing a job one had held for several years and come to rely on. But sometimes the shock can require a minor readjustment so that life can return to its "normal" routine.

Whether it is a big or a small shock, we have the ability and the faculty to deal with it and to move on. According to the saying, "What doesn't kill us makes us stronger," we can overcome shocks and become more resilient in the future. Perhaps even what will kill us (and something eventually will) has the possibility of making us stronger, more understanding and more resilient. For example, if we receive the news that we are suffering from an incurable illness, we still have the opportunity to deal with this news in a way that will strengthen our character and afford us the opportunity to proceed with dignity and forbearance.

A shock is like a propulsion that allows a person to take two steps ahead into the unknown, rather than proceeding along established and familiar paths one step at a time.

Shocks are unavoidable—there will always be some jolts that will promote new ways of viewing our life, and the current situation we are in. They are a leap into the future and into stormy weather. Shocks can also be associated with spontaneous healing and great beneficial changes in your life.

This hexagram is a warning about obstacles or changes ahead. Although life and every day bring about continuous changes, a shock is more dramatic, bringing about change within a shorter period of time.

The Oracle says:
Build shock absorbers into your life by always expecting the unexpected.

Exercise:
Think of the times in your life when you have experienced a shock. Maybe it was an accident, a sudden death in the family, or the unexpected end of a relationship. What happened next? What did the shock lead to? Was the change beneficial in the long run?

52. SERENITY
Mountain below, Mountain above

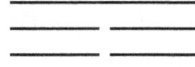

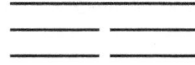

As in the famous prayer, the quality of serenity becomes available when one settles to accept what cannot be changed, but strives to change what can be changed for the better. It is a fine balance between the two states, and the skill lies in recognizing the difference between the two.

If we try to change what cannot be changed, we become frustrated, and it can impair our self-view; if we do not change what can be changed for the better, we will live a life that will be lesser in its quality and opportunities. When one discovers this place within which serenity resides, it brings with it an equanimity within which a person can deal with anything that might come along to challenge one's sanity.

Do not expect to always live in the place of serenity; it is a continuous journey to find it, touch it, and then move on. Living a life allows us glimpses of serenity when our journey feels in balance and on track. But soon something will inevitably come to disrupt the perceived harmony and bring us into a state of hesitancy, wherein we do not know what our next step or action should be.

The image that goes with this hexagram is that of a mountain below and a mountain above. This is the place of serenity: there is a mountain that has been climbed, and the journey offers now a vision of the next mountain to be tackled. We are well equipped for this next challenge; it is simply a matter of taking each day one at a time and putting our best foot forward, carefully so as not to slip back and lose the elevation we have worked so hard to attain.

Wherever you are in your journey, rejoice because you are

alive, and as long as you are within your energetic bubble, called the aura, there is much you can do and still achieve. Look back at the mountain you have just climbed and see if it suggests to you the nature of the journey that is still ahead of you. Look forward to the mountain yet to be ascended and see if it also suggests to you the nature of the journey still ahead of you. What are your special talents and how can you share them with others?

This hexagram suggests you take this moment to think of the kind of legacy you would like to leave behind when you depart from this body you now inhabit.

The Oracle says:
Serenity awaits you if you can discover what it is that you have come into this life to achieve.

Exercise:
Write down three words or phrases to describe the high points of your journey so far. Looking ahead, find three words or phrases to describe what you would still like to achieve in this lifetime.

53. GRADUAL PROGRESS
Mountain below, Wind above

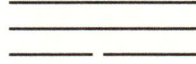

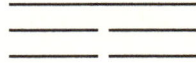

G radual progress is best. Progress that is sudden, unexpected and not worked for has not had a chance to establish firm foundations and could be short-lived. It is like winning the lottery. It is a known fact that people who unexpectedly come into an inheritance of some kind, or win a large amount of money in a game, or by playing the lottery, soon lose what they have gained.

Do not be impatient when waiting to see results of your labor. Every action that you make has an opposite reaction, and the timings are unpredictable. No matter how distant the future, it is already on its way now. Results are coming; it may seem that the returns for your efforts are slow in arriving, but your perceived timing is not the same as universal timing. So be patient, and in the meantime, while waiting for results of past efforts, invest new efforts for future results.

Everything you do is written down in the worlds of energy; we paint our own portrait as we live day by day. Every moment is a new brush stroke; every day a new color is added to our life's palette. Gradual progress will last longer than fast progress. It takes nine months for a baby to fully form within the womb; likewise it takes years to fully build the character we would want to have and be known for by others.

Life is a learning, and in a way, this planet is our classroom. We learn from nature, as well as from books and the experiences of others. Every day the store of knowledge recorded in the energy worlds of this planet as well as in the written records and oral traditions increases. We are recipients of that knowledge as well as contributors. Every time we have an "aha" moment, it is recorded in the astral record and from there is then available to all forever, or as long as this planet continues to exist with its recorded history written indelibly into its aura, also known as its energy fields.

Life itself is a gradual progress through time. If we can make it work for us, we will complete this journey on Earth as a better person and our next incarnation, if it is to be here on this planet, can be even better than this one, with many opportunities to share our gifts and to support others.

This hexagram is a reminder that life is a journey and that we are always given the opportunity to become an important participant in human evolution.

The Oracle says:
You are an instrument of Creation. Can you say what that
instrument can best do?

Exercise:
Ask yourself each day, how can you become a better person so that as the sun goes down in the evening you can say how you will have contributed to the human story and the gradual progress of your own development.

54. MARRYING
Lake below, Thunder above

arriage is a commitment, either to another person or to an idea, or to a way of life. Queen Elizabeth the First said she was married to the country and did not need to marry a man. Marriage is the bringing together of two of almost anything. Off the coast of Japan there are two rocks that were married by the local people long ago, due to their similarity and proximity. There is a rope joining them together and this rope has been renewed by local people for centuries, as soon as it deteriorates due to its exposure to wind, water and salt.

In a temple in Japan two trees are joined together by a rope, much the same way as the rocks had been married long ago. In our lifetime we might become married to another person, but we might also become committed and married to an idea, a religion, a belief system, a theory, or a cause. It is natural for a human to commit to someone or something, but it is also natural to be afraid of commitment because commitment limits our freedom. We value our freedom, and perhaps we do not realize that we are never truly free because we are always subject to the laws of the universe and the laws of man. There is a seeming contradiction here, in that the greatest freedom can be earned by the greatest commitment to the ways of the universe.

Commitment takes time. Marriage occurs after a period of engagement during which two people get to know each other and decide whether they want to commit to living together and sharing their lives for years to come—perhaps to the end of their lives. Marriage is always confirmed by witnesses and legally registered in the town hall or wherever such documents are kept. Marriage affects the families involved, as their members get to know each other due to the commitment made by the newlyweds. Marriage is also a declaration of intent as a person says their vows and commits to another person.

It is easy to physically see the commitment to marriage if the person involved is wearing a wedding ring. Some Catholic nuns and sisters wear a silver ring to show their commitment to God and the church. We tend to develop many relationships and commitments throughout our lives.

The question this hexagram asks is, what are you committed to?

The Oracle says:
A responsible person commits to fulfill their obligations. Be prompt in your responses to the needs of those you have committed to.

Exercise:
Decide who or what you want to commit to and write your vows confirming your commitment.

55. ABUNDANCE
Fire below, Thunder above

What is the greatest achievement a person can rise to while living here on Earth? Is it fame and fortune? Is it a meaningful relationship? Or is it being content and happy with what one has, whatever that might be?

If you were given a blank check and told you could fill it in with any number, what would that number be? And once you decided on a number, what would you do with all that money? Do you know? Have you thought about it? Would you help others? Would you move to a better home and location? Would you quit your job? Would you buy a new car, or yacht, or plane? Would you make your life more complicated by having to look after a series of possessions or by having to pay servants?

What is your greatest desire? Is it fame, or health, or wealth? And if you could have everything your heart desired, what would be your next goal? What would you do for the rest of your life? Do you have an aim that can take you beyond success and still give you a path forward in life? One of the secrets how to have abundance is to develop the long view so you never completely rest or feel you have achieved everything you wanted in life.

Rock stars who achieve fame and wealth in their life when they are still young often pay the price of their achievements by becoming disillusioned with life and end up taking drugs, abusing alcohol and having many temporary relationships. A sportsperson who achieves the highest accolades in their chosen discipline have nothing further to aim for and might not have the incentive to keep going and to continue to try to improve.

If you imagine all you every wanted coming to pass, what would you next wish for? Where would success then take you? There is one goal and one desire that can last a lifetime, and that is continuance. Even if we achieve everything we had ever desired, we can always wish for it to continue.

The author once wished for a new job and I made a list of everything I wanted—more pay, a pleasant boss, a gym nearby, an office closer to home. As soon as I had made my list I found the ideal job, and the gym was in the same building as the office so I could easily exercise during my lunch breaks. However, I never asked for it to continue and within six months the team I was working with was downsized and I lost my ideal job.

This hexagram says that abundance is possible, but asks the question, what will you do with it once you have it?

The Oracle says:
Appreciate what you already have, and when you experience abundance, remember to share it with others.

Exercise:
Write down what you want. It is the first step toward materializing your desires.

56. TRAVELING
Mountain below, Fire above

When setting out on a journey, you are surrendering to a new set of rules that can be quite different from the ones you are used to abiding by in your day by day life. You have far less control over external circumstances, as planes, buses, and trains are often delayed, and cars can break down. You become subject to schedules and the capriciousness of inanimate objects. You might say that you are forced to surrender to the gods of the road.

So when planning a journey, it is important to pack up and take with you your best attempt at equanimity and patience. If a car breaks down, you need to wait for help to arrive; if a plane is late, you need to wait until it is ready to depart; if you miss the bus, you need to wait for the next one. It is in these circumstances that you need to be able to think and plan your next steps with clarity and forethought. There might be, for example, another available flight or an Uber ride that can take you to your chosen destination. This is not a time to get upset with the fact that your journey has been so rudely interrupted; it is a time to take sensible and available action.

Traveling offers an opportunity to leave behind your routines and habitual ways—it encourages you to look up and around you and see the new vistas unfolding before you with childlike curiosity and wonder. It encourages you to meet new people and appreciate different customs; it teaches you new languages and introduces new and exotic cuisines. It causes your senses to become more alert, alive and astute. It is an opportunity to learn new behaviors and make new friends.

Most people travel at some time in their life—sometimes out of necessity, sometimes for work, and sometimes for pleasure. Whatever the reason for your excursions, try to make the most of your travels and new experiences. Enjoy the four parts to every journey: preparation, leaving home, being there and coming back. Each has its own gifts to impart and lessons to teach.

This hexagram says that life is a journey and it, too, has its own rules. We discover what works and what does not as we grow and age. Every stage of the journey is better if we are able to approach it with serenity: accepting what we cannot change and changing what we can.

The Oracle says:
Within the larger journey of life there are many small journeys to learn from and enjoy.

Exercise:
Write a bucket list—where would you like to go and what would you like to see? Make plans to organize one item on your list.

57. THE PENETRATING WIND
Wind below, Wind above

The winds of change are blowing into your life and into everybody else's life as well. Nothing stays the same for long. Think of the city, town or village where you grew up. Does that place exist anymore, or has it changed almost beyond recognition? Where are the children you went to school with? They have grown up and probably have children of their own. Where are your grandparents or great grandparents? Some of them have probably departed. As time moves on, people enter and leave through the revolving doors of the planet.

Look at a picture from your childhood, and then look at the mirror. What has changed? How many experiences have you collected to yourself throughout the years; how many relationships have you forged? How many hellos and goodbyes have you uttered throughout your life? However many there have been, there are more to come.

Everyone is growing older, as we age, too. It is a comforting thought that an older brother or sister will always be older and a younger one will be younger, as long as we and they live. As we age we become historians of the era of our childhood and youth, and some changes we tell our children or younger friends about, often cause marvel or disbelief. A world without the Internet? How could that be? No phones? How was that possible? You had to carry your suitcase because it had no wheels? What were people thinking back then?

Every little change in our living circumstances had to be invented and implemented, and each has a story to tell. The first airplane, the first train, the first car, the first toilet. Most people have heard of the Wright brothers, but probably few have heard of Sir John Harington, the godson of Queen Elizabeth the First who was the inventor of the first flushable toilet.

Change keeps us humans on our toes, as we can never completely settle for what we have and where we are—our natural instinct drives us forward. Although sometimes the results of such changes can be seen as regression, we can always keep looking on the bright side of life.

This hexagram says that you are in flux and will not remain the same—tomorrow you will be different. The question is, will it be a better you?

The Oracle says:
Embrace change. It is your friend.

Exercise:
Write down the decades you have lived through in your life: childhood, adolescence, youth, mid-life, pre-menopause or pre-andropause, seniority and old age. Write down a word or phrase to describe each one you have been through. Contemplate the changes you have been through as you grew older, as well as the ones yet to come.

58. JOY
Lake below, Lake above

J oy is a powerful emotion and driving force. Cherish it. Learn to connect to joy at will when you discover what causes joy in your life. It could be an activity, like painting or writing, or it could be spending time with family or friends. Joy is everywhere and can be connected to by taking a walk in the park or listening to beautiful music, or simply recalling what one is grateful for.

Joy is a healer and an uplifter of spirits. Ask yourself, what brings you joy. Once you know what these activities are, try to make more time for them in your life. You deserve to have more joy and to be known to be accompanied by joy wherever you go.

Joy is like a guiding light—when it is present it indicates times when a person's life is on track—nothing is missing and no desires are unfulfilled. Joy is a settlement and a knowing that all is well.

Joy can be felt in any circumstance; even within the most horrific experiences one can be overcome with joy. Joy can come at the most unexpected times—it can seize one without warning or provocation. At those moments it is a reminder that being alive is a precious gift and that one has mighty friends—other people, the planet, the solar system, nature and the universe. Joy lifts a person up into higher energy realms where worry ceases and pain gives way. It is a medicine of the gods that alleviates suffering and causes a person to become noble and rich beyond measure.

Joy has inspired some great works of art, such as the *Ode to Joy* by Beethoven, a choir piece featured in his Ninth Symphony. C. S.

161

Lewis wrote the book, *Surprised by Joy: the Shape of My Early Life* in which he describes his youthful journey from childhood, and loss of his mother, to boarding school in England, to the trenches of World War One and to Oxford where he made the decision to embrace the Christian faith. Like Lewis, many people associate joy with their belief in a higher power and with their conviction that they are loved and looked after within a purposeful universe.

Joy is indeed often a surprise because it lives in unexpected places. When we pursue it, it often escapes us. But when we are simply happy to be who we are, to be with whoever we are with, and to fully be where we are, joy has a habit of materializing in a shower of gratitude and peace. It enhances a person's day—when it is present, everything looks more beautiful. Colors are brighter, people are more courteous and opportunities unfold before one, as if by magic.

The word joy can also be found in such words as enjoyment and joyful. You enjoy something that brings joy into your life and into your energy field. We enjoy what we love to do; we can also enjoy the results of another person's creative work, like a book, a movie, or a performance. Joy can be found everywhere—in the beauty of nature or in the works of man. The key to finding joy is developing the eyes to see it, the ears to hear it, and the sensitivity to feel it.

Happiness tends to be fleeting, but joy can be a constant companion. It is a state of mind and it accompanies one's belief in the purposefulness of Creation and one's role within it. To enter the kingdom of joy one has a decision to make: does the universe support your life and provide you with everything the human needs to continue living? Or do you live in a hostile universe? Once this fundamental question is answered and you decide you live in a gentle, benevolent, and friendly universe, joy will be waiting to join you on your journey through life, wherever it takes you.

Joy comes from the sense of connection to energies bigger and more powerful than us. It comes from universal acceptance, which is always there, but rarely felt or appreciated. Joy connects us to a greater purpose within which we can play a significant part. It confirms our importance and our humanity; it allows a person to learn from the most challenging adversities and to always have hope, no matter what the circumstance.

With joy, all becomes possible. A joyful person becomes powerful and comfortable in their own skin. They believe in themselves and in the fact that they have a unique destiny to fulfill. With joy there is a sense of belonging—we are here for a reason, not for self gratification or personal gain. Our joyful tasking is to find out what this purpose is and to align our thoughts, actions and feelings to that purpose.

Joy brings with it the understanding and the acceptance that the planet is our temporary home and that there are other worlds where joy is a way of life. This planet could be a world of joy if each person followed their dream and their calling, and filled themselves and their energy field with joy.

This hexagram alerts you to the ubiquity of joy and suggests you develop the senses to see it, hear it and feel it.

The Oracle says:
When you love your life, joy will accompany you and open your eyes to the beauty all around you.

Exercise:
Write down what gives you joy and make an attempt to increase the time you spend enjoying what you do.

59. DISPERSION
Water below, Wind above

I n this day and age it is easy to become dispersed. There are so many aspects of our life today that vie for our attention. Advertising has become a major part of our life, screaming at us incessantly from the television screen, from magazines, from our computers, for billboards and from shop windows. Then there are all the chores that need to be looked after during each day—there is work, family, relationships, entertainment, study, travel, and so much more. It is difficult not to become dispersed and overwhelmed.

Most people suffer from dispersion most of the time. They start something, only for their attention to be drawn elsewhere. Sometimes they might even forget what they had started until much later when they come across a job that was initiated but never finished.

An antidote to dispersion is focus. It is an important skill in this day and age to be able to focus one's attention and keep it focused. To do so, one needs to be able to draw boundaries for oneself and to be able to say no to that which attempts to distract one from one's chosen path.

We all have many projects and many initiatives on the go. It is in a way natural in these times to be interested in many things and to be able to pursue many interests. We have access to just about every book that has ever been written via the Internet and we can look up information on almost anyone who has ever achieved any modicum of fame within seconds. We can communicate across the world instantaneously and the availability of Skype and FaceTime has given us the ability to speak with people over long distance while watching their reactions in almost real time.

Another way to look at dispersion is to understand that every human is a dispersion field of energy and that the moment we focus our attention on someone or something, we connect to it and some of our energy travels toward them, while we receive a bit of their energy as well.

This hexagram advises us to be conscious of those people and things we connect to and to limit our connections to situations which can drain us of energy.

The Oracle says:
You are not only physical beings, but you are processors and distributors of energy. Be careful what you give your energy to and be aware of the influence people you meet have upon you.

Exercise:
Think back to the past week. Who were the people you met or spent time with? Can you describe the influence they had upon you—was it enhancing or draining?

60. LIMITATION
Lake below, Water above

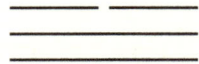

This hexagram points to the need for moderation in everything. Virtually everything taken or consumed in excess amounts is bad for you. We are made to eat, drink and take in energy within limits. We have a limited capacity for intake.

There are two states that we alternate between—taking in and giving out. We breathe in and we breathe out. We listen and we speak. We eat and we excrete. We do not do both these actions at the same time.

Everything around us has its limits, even the planet. But the human potential knows no boundaries. We can reach the stars with our mind and travel outside the planet with our imagination. What is faster than the speed of light? The speed of thought. We can reach the other side of the planet in a split second.

Every year sport records are broken, as someone demonstrates that a new, better result is possible. So, on the one hand we are limited in our physicality—for example, we cannot fly without a plane or balloon—but on the other, we do not know where the limits of our potential are.

Remote viewing is the ability to connect to places and people at a distance. It has been used and developed by the military, both in Russia and the United States. It was said of Lord Nelson that "he was in his hammock and a thousand miles away." Somehow he was always able to find the French navy and attack when they least expected him.

It is natural for a human to have premonition, or to be able to foretell the future, or to see what others cannot see within the realms of energy. There are countless records and examples of people breaking through barriers and establishing new norms of possibility. The first requirement to develop these extra-sensory abilities is to believe that it is possible. Some skills require training and knowledge, whereas others sometimes just happen and make themselves known. There are stories of people suddenly discovering that they have healing abilities, or being hit by lightning and finding they can now play the piano masterfully and with ease.* This means that quantum leaps in one's abilities and skills are possible.

This hexagram reminds us that as humans we are on a development journey and can always improve in everything we do, if we implement our time and efforts to make this a reality.

The Oracle says:
Moderation on the one hand and greater efforts are needed on the other; find your way and decide which is required from you in your life's journey.

Exercise:
Write down examples of times when you have been clairvoyant, or when you were able to predict the future, or when you connected with empathy to someone else's feelings or pain. Ask your faculty to deliver to you more such moments and abilities.

In 1994, when Tony Cicoria was 42 years old, he was struck by lightning near Albany, New York, while standing next to a public telephone. Then Cicoria, over a period of two or three days, became struck with an insatiable desire to listen to piano music. He acquired a piano and started to teach himself to play. His head was flooded with music that seemed to come from nowhere. Although before his accident, he had had no particular interest in music, within three months of being struck by lightning Cicoria spent nearly all his time playing and composing.

61. INNER TRUTH
Lake below, Wind above

Every person has their inner truth. This is what they believe in and what they know in their hearts to be true. It might not be an objective truth, someone else might hold to a completely different truth and both are convinced they are right.

Even if we watch a television recording of an event, we still might not be seeing the truth and the whole truth. The camera will record one angle of vision; it has its limitations and depending on the person operating the camera, it will have its own bias. Even if you had a dozen cameras recording an event from twelve angles, you would still not be able to record the whole truth of the event. There would always be something missing—some sleight of hand, a fly passing across the table, or a brief smile flitting around the corner of someone's mouth.

We can only know our truth and try to be as objective and as faithful to it as we can be. It would be easy to accept what we want to accept as the truth; it is much harder to not settle for one's own biases, but to always verify the truth with the experiences of others and with the witnesses to our experiences, victories and struggles.

Truth is not only about events and past experience, but the greatest truth we can define is the decision as to who we really are and who we are going to become.

Everyone has their belief about what happens to us when we die. We might have our faith which gives us one interpretation of life after death; we might have read books in which there are accounts by people who have had near death experiences and have come back to share those experiences. We might have read and heard ghost stories and wondered whether the soul or spirit stays around the place where it had lived and died. We might have read the *Egyptian Book of the Dead** or the *Tibetan Book of the Dead*** (both of which had different titles when they were first published). There are so many truths surrounding life after death, it is sometimes difficult to separate the truth from the falsehoods. As long as we are alive it is our duty to keep searching for the truth of our existence and to be open to get rid of our inner truth if it no longer fits with what we know to be true.

This hexagram challenges you to re-examine your beliefs, so that you can be open when a new truth contradicting the one you have held as true previously presents itself to you.

The Oracle says:
There is not your truth or anybody's truth. There is only THE truth.

Exercise:
Write down what you think happens after death. Make a note to re-look at this writing in a year's time and see if your belief has changed, and if so, how and why.

---

* Originally titled *The Book of Going Forth by Day.*
** Originally titled *Liberation Through Hearing During the Intermediate State.*

62. MINOR ACHIEVEMENT
Mountain below, Thunder above

Small achievements cannot be overestimated. All great achievements consist of or follow on from thousands of small ones. No one has achieved success in one go. It takes many small efforts, all pointing in the same direction to become a great person. The small victories might go by unconfirmed and unnoticed, but they add up (or can add up) to become something great. So although it does not look like much at the time, a small achievement has the making of becoming a great success. Follow the trail of small successes and they will point the way toward a land of fame and fortune.

The big success has the habit of making a big splash and then petering out. But if it is supported by a trail of small successes, it will have a much greater chance of becoming a permanent feature within a person's life. Go small to go big, because if you aim to go big straight off the bat, you will end up small.

Have the big vision before you and take one step at a time. Each step will bring you closer to your goal. If you know where you are heading you can identify the small steps you need to take to progress upon the way.

They say that a journey of a thousand miles begins with a single step. Having taken that step, one needs to place the other foot in front of the first one, and keep repeating this action, so step three follows step two; step four follows step three and so on.

Sometimes it is possible to take a quantum leap forward. However, this hexagram speaks of the small steps and the hard work of continuance and being able to go on. It recommends small, deliberate actions and promises that such actions will bring success in the end. Persistence is a quality that brings results and ensures success.

If a life's journey consists of taking two steps forward and then one back, it means that the first step is only covered once, but each consequent step needs to be covered three times. Beginner's luck is an incentive and boost, but later needs to be matched with continuing effort and a slower pace while making progress. A slower speed is also useful when making mistakes or when it seems that results are not forthcoming.

This hexagram reminds us that patience is a virtue and that small efforts that do not immediately bring visible results can add up to a major success in the end.

The Oracle says:
Love the struggle because the fact that you have an aim and a goal gives your life meaning.

Exercise:
Imagine that your journey toward your goal is like a road trip. Can you name the towns that you need to pass on the way, so that you divide the journey into smaller, achievable chunks?

63. ACCOMPLISHMENT
Fire below, Water above

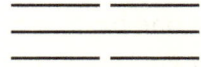

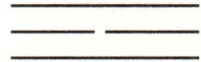

Once success is achieved, it is time to look around for the next aim or tasking. One needs to constantly have one's eyes on the end result so as not to settle for temporary success. Once a person achieves a trophy that perhaps they had coveted for a long time, the danger they face is that of atrophy, because now they are in danger of resting on their laurels and believing they no longer need to to try to keep growing and refining.

Being alive in these changing times is an accomplishment in itself. It means having survived nine months in the womb, having gone through the growing pains of childhood and the discoveries of adolescence. It means living in a culture that has its own demands; it means finding one's way in the world to be able to feed the body and nourish the soul.

Then there are the accomplishments that each unique person on Earth has achieved throughout their life. These are the things they have learned and the skills they have acquired, the qualities that have become part of their character formation, and the friendships and relationships they have developed over the years.

Mostly people tend to underestimate their accomplishments and achievements. Sometimes it is good to stop for a moment to value, for example, the ability to read and write, or the freedom that driving a car affords one. Think for a moment what it was like before the inventions of the telephone and the computer, or how difficult it was to travel before the invention of the airplane.

We take a lot of what is given to us in our life for granted, and tend to value it only after it is taken away or we lose it for whatever reason. Most people are born into a home and a family, and are well taken care of as they grow up. They go to school where they learn essential skills and acquire basic knowledge. These are important accomplishments which we add to later in life when we go out into the world to become independent and establish our own family.

This hexagram warns you against becoming too satisfied with your accomplishments and advises you to be grateful for what you already have achieved.

The Oracle says:
Whatever you have achieved today, tomorrow there is more to do!

Exercise:
Write a list of the skills you have acquired in your life. Then add five new skills you would like to gain in the next five years.

64. STRIVING
Water below, Fire above

I t has been said that "a woman's work is never done." There is always more to do: as a new day starts, there is food to be prepared, clothes to be washed, a home to be cleaned, a family to be looked after. It could also be said that a human's work is never done, because as long as we live there is more to be done. It is important never to stop and to always have something going on, some poker in the fire, some finger in the pie. We need our goals, our aims, our visions to keep us going, to keep us healthy and to keep us on the right track. Life is a journey and we are travelers. The moment we stop and rest by the way, we are not standing still; we are regressing.

Sometimes, as people get older and retire from work, they lose their sense of purpose. This could be a recipe for disaster. A person who is no longer interested in living is hurtling toward the exit. To prolong your life, it is important to be involved, to have plans, desires and aims. But not all goals are equal; some of our desires might appear to be selfish. The universe recognizes helping others as an important contribution to life on Earth. Self-improvement, learning and developing new skills are also aims that can resonate within the worlds of energy and the angelic realms. If you think you need help in navigating life and keeping healthy, it might be a good idea to petition for help, so that you can be supported as you strive to become co-creator with the higher powers that are influential here on this planet.

As long as we are alive here on Earth there is more to do. There are always people who need help or a friend to talk to. We are here to share our time together, to support one another and to promote each other. It is a known fact that people who have a family or a community to share with tend to live longer. Being alive is being employed by the universe. We are here for a reason, and sometimes it takes time to work out what exactly that reason is.

When something is fulfilled, it is finished and its work is done. You are not finished, but are still work in progress. You can continue to add colorful strokes to your emerging portrait. Human evolution is still happening and there is a lot of development we have yet to achieve—our brain has much room to grow into and our extra-sensory perceptions are still in their infancy stages.

This hexagram is an invitation to continue striving for perfection. As long as we live on Earth we will not achieve perfection, but at any given moment we can be the best we can be.

The Oracle says:
Become a co-creator with god and the angels. Help this planet help the human race in its evolutionary journey.

Exercise:
Write down all the tasks you fulfill during any single week. If there is anything you could use some help with, decide to ask—whether another person or the universe.

www.ingramcontent.com/pod-product-compliance
Lightning Source LLC
Chambersburg PA
CBHW020859090426
42736CB00008B/433